Dominique Lecourt

London: NLB

Atlantic Highlands: HUMANITIES PRESS

Proletarian Science?

The Case of Lysenko

Introduction by Louis Althusser

Translated by Ben Brewster

Library of Congress Cataloging in Publication Data

Lecourt, Dominique.
  Proletarian science?

  Translation of Lyssenko.
  Includes index.
  1. Lysenko, Trofim Denisovich, 1898–1976. 2. Geneticists – Russia –
Biography. 3. Agriculturists – Russia – Biography. 4. Biology – History. I. Title.
QH31.L95L413   575'.0092'4 [B]   77-23002
ISBN 0-391-00738-6

First published as *Lyssenko*
by François Maspero, 1976

©François Maspero, 1976

This edition first published 1977

©NLB, 1977

Designed by Ruth Prentice

Filmset in 11 on 12 pt. 'Monophoto' Bembo by
Servis Filmsetting Ltd, Manchester

Printed in Great Britain by
Lowe and Brydone Printers Ltd, Norfolk

Bound by Kemp Hall Bindery, Oxford

ISBN 902308 69 6

Contents

Louis Althusser

Unfinished History

It is nowadays child's play to deal with the problem of Lysenko, dismissing him as a charlatan whose fortune was entirely bound up with Stalin's despotism. But it is a much more perilous enterprise to examine the history of Lysenkoism from a Marxist standpoint.

Here I will restrict myself to a few remarks, to some glaring facts and memories.

There is, after all, something curious about this long and tumultuous adventure of Lysenko, an adventure which covers nearly fifty years of Soviet history, which mobilized successively the forces of the agricultural apparatus, then those of the official philosophy and, finally, in the great consecration of 1948, the Soviet state apparatus and all the world's Communists – a long, scandalous and dramatic history which, over a period of decades, and on the basis of a theoretical fraud, produced confrontations, splits, tragedies and victims: *this history simply does not exist.*

It sleeps in the silence of closed Soviet archives, in the fact that, theoretically and politically, it has already been buried. It does, it is true, still haunt the memory of those who survived the repression and the blackmail, but no Soviet philosopher or scientist has raised, or has been able to raise his voice in order to write a Marxist history of this period, and shed a little light into the shadows.[1] The silence of the Soviets, who hold the archives, is paralleled by that of the Communists who, outside of the Soviet Union, have lived through the same constraints of the same history, and are keeping quiet about it.

An extraordinary paradox thus asserts itself here, just as it does in the case of the terrible reality later baptized with the derisory

[1] Zh. Medvedev's book cannot, in spite of its interest, be described as a *Marxist* history.

name of the 'personality cult',[2] and in many other episodes in the history of the labour movement: the Communist Parties, provided by Marx for the first time in history with scientific means of understanding history, which they generally put to good use when analyzing other forces and other times, *seem to be powerless to account, as Marxists, for their own history* – especially when they have made a mistake.

It is no good to argue that it is difficult to orient oneself in history, that the strongest will can be overwhelmed by the conditions and lose its way, that the past, tradition, habit (Lenin feared them all) can cast their shadow over the present. Because these conditions can themselves be analyzed (if new concepts are needed for the task, why are they not produced?). And, finally, supposing that this analysis is neglected, the murkiest history is nevertheless clear enough in its effects for Communists to recognize, even in their silence, *by the fact* that rectifications have taken place (of this or that detail or line), *the fact* of their error.

But, it will be said, if the mistake has been rectified, what does it matter that Communists turn their back on it, provided that they are 'advancing'? Have the Soviets not themselves 'rectified' the 'violations of Soviet legality' to which the system called the 'personality cult' is apparently to be reduced? Have they not 'rectified' the errors of Lysenkoism by giving the geneticists their jobs back and re-establishing their tarnished reputations? And the French Communist Party, which more than any other had marched forward, its leaders sheltered behind its 'great intellectuals', exalting Lysenkoism and the theory of the 'two sciences', bourgeois and proletarian – has it not 'put matters right' by abandoning, at the right moment, its professions of faith, and by ceasing to pressurize its militants? No-one has explained himself, of course. But that really does not matter, because in any case things have been 'put right'. . . . And, to crown this 'argument', it is always possible to invoke a good, tailor-made theory of the primacy of practice over theory: a concrete act is worth more than all the analyses in the world!

It must be said without hesitation that this whole argument is unworthy of Marxism. Remember Lenin, who (be it said for all Popperian lovers of 'falsification') alloted to *error* a privileged role

---

[2] With two exceptions: F. Claudin, *The Communist Movement*; C. Bettelheim, *Les Luttes de classes en U.R.S.S.*

in the process of the rectification of knowledge, to the point where he conferred on it, with respect to scientific experiment and political practice, a kind of heuristic primacy over 'truth': how many times did he repeat that it is worse to blind yourself and keep silent about a defeat than to suffer it, that it is worse to close your eyes to an error than to commit it.

And we know how often he had to admit such an error: over Brest-Litovsk, the conditions of which he never ceased to examine; over war communism: 'we were wrong', and here is why . . . Lenin was not a historian, but, from his action station, faced with the terrible contradictions of the Soviet Revolution, he warned that the labour movement must analyze and understand its past, not out of a love of historical study but for *political* reasons related to the present itself: so that it will not be fighting in the dark. You must go to the root of things, analyze the reasons for an error in order to *understand* it properly and thus really to be able to rectify it: if you do not, then even in the most favourable of cases you will only put it right in part, and a superficial part at that. Lenin had a quite different idea of putting things right from this notion of a circumstantial 'rectification'. In pleading for the primacy of analysis, in arguing the need for the labour movement to understand its own history, what it had *done*, where it had succeeded and where it had failed, he was pleading for the *primacy of Marxist politics*.

This question of the way to treat mistakes must be very seriously considered if we are to weigh up what Lenin meant when he said that to close your eyes to an error is worse than to commit it.

For we know, we who have no religion, not even the religion of our theory, still less that of the goals of history, that the class struggle is never crystal-clear, and that the proletariat, which fights its own class struggle, a different one from the struggle of the bourgeoisie, is not transparent to itself, a composite class, always engaged in forging its unity. It is in the class struggle that the proletariat comes to disentangle and confront the relations of forces in which it is enmeshed, and succeeds in defining the 'line' of its struggle. None of this resembles the clarity of the case in which a pure consciousness confronts the pure objectivity of a situation. For the whole process is constituted and dominated by contradictory relations which are only realized and discovered little by little, and may later reveal some surprises, either of anticipation (overdetermination) or of retardation (underdetermination). That is why, inserted as it is in a dominant system of relations, the class struggle is necessarily a history full of errors, sometimes dramatic or tragic. The possibility of such errors, just like the possibility of deviations, is written into the contradictory relations dominating the class struggle. An error – even if it has been pointed out in advance by a neglected, disowned, disarmed or defeated minority – is always recognized and denounced as an error (if it *is* recognized!) when it is already *too late*. And since this struggle develops, even for those who have seen clearly in advance, without the aid of any superior instance judging and deciding each question, we must speak here, paradoxically, of *error without truth* and of *deviation without a norm*. An unmastered fault, a hesitation, aberration, defeat or crisis, which slowly develops or suddenly gapes in the midst of reality, a reality without truth or norm: that is error, that is deviation.

To return to Lenin: is it sufficient to recognize, after the event, the existence of an error (or of a deviation) and to content oneself with 'rectifying' it in silence, without setting oneself the task, as a Marxist, of analyzing its real history, that is, its conditions and causes? I say no. If the party, faced with a real mistake, with an error which can no longer be tolerated, is content simply to recognize it and 'rectify' it without explaining it, *i.e.*, without subjecting it to a real and profound Marxist analysis, then the substance of the error will quite simply persist, sheltered by this silence, in its 'rectified' form. How can an error be rectified if you refuse to talk about its history, to analyze it, to try to understand it? How can you seriously claim to have 'rectified' an error *which you have not understood?* You are condemned to 'rectify', arbitrarily, only its most easily visible aspects, or, which is the most invidious, only details or surface elements. In short, you will 'make amends for things' – but only in so far as that is possible without troubling the established order, which needs nothing more than silence. When no-one will talk about an error, then the error remains. Even supposing that it was not 'rectified' just a little bit *in order* for it to be allowed to live on in peace.

It is clear that in these matters the frontier between error, disingenuity and deceit is very tenuous: blindness to the sources of error, whether such blindness is intentional or simply tolerated, is usually *politically* inspired. If Lenin attached so much importance to dealing with error, it is because *the process of dealing with error is always a political process*, and implies a political struggle. The test of time has shown that there is no third way: just as an act of political determination is required in order to destroy error and its roots, so an act of political determination is required – even if it is not open, but hidden – in order *not* to analyze it, *not* to understand it and therefore *not* to root it out: a determination to take the side of error, to promote the political cause which wants that error to live on in peace.

Must we once again refer to the reality designated by the notorious term: 'the personality cult'? Yes, we must – because the silence has not yet been broken. But why object to the burial of such long-lasting and tragic facts, even if they have not been explained? Did not the 20th Congress of the Soviet Party in any case admit the 'error' (and, it is often added: what other party in the world has ever dared to make such an admission?) and 'rectify' it? Has not 'socialist legality' been restored (having 'simply' been violated)? Have not the Soviet leaders thus 'put matters right', corrected the 'abuses'? All those voices which pointed out the error in advance were of course silenced by abuse, punishment, even death. But the moment came when, the crisis having become open, the error had to be admitted. It was thus admitted after the event, and in a very limited, very circumscribed fashion, and dealt with in terms of a few limited decisions which were decreed to be adequate. But as far as the search for its basic causes is concerned – for its roots in the history of the Soviet social formation, in the class struggles of that formation, and in the political 'line' applied in the infrastructure and superstructure: silence. I am not talking about the silence or half-silence of the moment, but about a silence which has lasted twenty years. It is clear that the Soviet leaders have refused *and are still refusing* to undertake a Marxist analysis of this gigantic error, buried, like its millions of victims, in official silence. They have even gone back on the few poor glimpses of elucidation with which Khrushchev awakened hope. The USSR thus lives on in symptomatic silence about its own history. It is a sure bet that this silence is not foreign to the system. Lenin's words echo again: to keep silent about an error means to allow or to encourage the error to persist. If the silence continues, then the error continues. The purpose of the silence may even be to *ensure* that it continues – in order to reap the ensuing political benefits.

I do not of course deny that the masses are no longer touched by its bloodiest forms, nor that it now claims an infinitely smaller number of direct victims; but it does still claim victims, and the repressive system of the Stalin period, including the camps, remains in existence, as do the basic practices of that period regarding social, political and cultural life. Behind these, there subsist the essential elements of an economism, coupled with its ideological counterpoint, a verbal humanism of a terribly conformist and ponderous kind. Shall we add an *a contrario* proof, which would be ridiculous if it were not so eloquent? In order to 'salvage' Soviet socialism before French public opinion, very responsible French Communist officials have explained to us that the 'difficulties' encountered by the Soviet Union in its transition to 'democratic socialism' are simply formal, since the USSR is only 'lagging behind' by 'socialist standards', that is, lagging behind itself. The proof? The USSR has all the '*resources*' (economic growth, widespread culture) needed to become fully 'democratic', and what is more, it feels the '*need*' to do so ('the need for extended democracy' – *sic*). What is missing, then? Strictly speaking, nothing. Just one extra little factor, the idea of 'democratic' socialism, which has not yet occurred to the Soviets, but which will occur: we must just wait *a little* longer. But the unfortunate fact, or rather, the *simple fact* is that the USSR manifestly does not want to know about this dialectic of backwardness, of the resources and need for democracy and the 'extra' little factor. Contrary to what we are told, and to this quite un-Marxist pseudo-dialectic, it is probable that the Soviet régime has neither the resources nor any need for 'democratic socialism'. If it has not really analyzed, in Marxist terms, the class basis of its gigantic historical 'error', that is certainly not because it is forgetful or absent-minded, but because somewhere, in its own social relations, there exists a *political* 'need' for this error, in order to maintain these relations, and thus a need for the error to live on, too. It is time to call a spade a spade, and stop telling (ourselves) stories. It has to be admitted that the reality which the Soviet leaders have refused and are still refusing to analyze in Marxist terms does constitute, in so far as it has not been 'rectified', an integral part of the Soviet system (and not a simple relic or accident), because it plays an essential political role within it. The subtlest distinctions or apologetic histories cannot change this fact. The substance of the practices of the Stalin period, unanalyzed, are peacefully pursuing their career in the USSR and elsewhere. It is crystal-clear that, if these practices have not been analyzed, it is for *political* reasons: so that they should not be exposed to danger, so that they should live on, for they are necessary to the maintenance of the existing social relations. But in that case the question must be completely re-framed, so as to get rid of the derisory theory of an 'accident' in 'time and space' – an accident which just happened to befall a socialism otherwise as imperturbable as an Aristotelian substance (the theory depends on the conceptual distinction: substance/accident). The simple but serious problem must be posed: *what social relations today constitute the Soviet social formation?*

The Lysenko episode is obviously in itself an episode of lesser historical weight. But the lesson which it teaches is no less important. And it has a direct interest for us, since the French Communist Party played a vanguard ideological and political role in the matter in the years 1948–52. Here too things have been 'rectified'. But how? Without any analysis. So what chance was there that anyone would get to the roots of the matter and attack its effects on the basis of a knowledge of its causes? The phenomenon was *reduced* to the one element which it was intended to 'rectify'. Just as the Soviets have reduced the facts of the Stalinian deviation to the purely juridical aspect of 'violations of socialist legality', so Lysenkoism was reduced to a theoretical folly involving questions of biology, a folly abetted by State intervention. Once the scientific position had been 'put right', once the theory of the 'two sciences' had been abandoned and State intervention in research forbidden, it was decided to pass on to 'next business' without any further explanation. Silence on the question of the social stratum of 'intellectuals' involved by this State ideology which bound them – by ties of pressure, threats and repression – to the State, whose domination over the popular masses they in turn served. Silence on the class relations and conflicts and on the political line, one of economism and voluntarism, which supported the whole system. And silence on the fact that the official version of dialectical materialism *guaranteed* Lysenko's theories, while these theories in turn served to '*verify*' this official version and to strengthen its pretension to the role of 'science of sciences'. The controlled 'rectification' of Lysenkoism did not touch on these realities, which nevertheless determined the historical destiny of this aberration.

They have pursued their career in the official silence which surrounds them.

I will select only one example among all those which exist: that of Marxist philosophy. So compromised was it, and visibly compromised, by the Lysenko episode, that the analysis of this error should have entailed its thoroughgoing examination. It would then have been possible to see that a certain, let us say *ontological* version of Marxist philosophy had for a number of years been gaining ground in the USSR, that it had been codified by Stalin in his famous chapter of the *History of the C.P.S.U.(B.),* and that it had become dominant in the Soviet Union and in all Communist Parties. It would have been possible to understand that certain previously existing contradictions of Marxist philosophy, which can be found in the writings of Marx and Engels, had allowed later writers, and finally Stalin, to rush headlong into an ontology. And it would thus have been possible to acquire some perspectives on a philosophy which presents the paradoxical characteristic of existing in a practical state in the theoretical and political deeds of the labour movement without ever being defined except in terms of certain cursory theses whose system remains, and for good reasons, problematical. In short, it would have been possible seriously to pose, from a Marxist standpoint, the question of dialectical materialism, of its contradictions and deviations, in order really to put Marxist philosophy onto its own road: a 'critical and revolutionary' road (Marx). But no. Things were left in their original state. And the dominant version of dialectical materialism, which transforms materialism into an ontology of matter whose 'laws' are supposed to be stated by the dialectic, the version which refuses to recognize that the whole virtue of materialism and of dialectics lies in the fact that they state not 'laws' but *theses* – this version has pursued its successful career. *Indeed, it remains dominant even today.* Negative and servile protests by Soviet philosophers and their followers – like their ridiculous warnings against 'deductivism' (*sic*), which remind one of 'wet paint' warning signs – can never provide an escape road from domination by a version of Marxist philosophy which remains totally aloof in its 'interpretation' of and apology for the *fait accompli*, and therefore quite reactionary and unproductive. Have Marxist philosophers forgotten what Marx said about dialectics, that it could become one thing or the other, could either become 'critical and revolutionary' or play the role of 'glorifying the existing state of affairs'?

And, to come to the political root of the question: why this silence, whose effect is to shelter and perpetuate the dominant version of Marxist philosophy? The reason must be that the profoundly conformist, apologetic function of this version, which excels in 'glorifying the existing state of affairs' and in transforming its practitioners into headmasters of the school of theoretical production, serves the existing political practices too well to be allowed to disappear: they 'need' it. In the best idealist tradition, which restricts itself to the work of 'interpreting' (Marx), it provides these practices in advance (that is, *after the event*) with a higher *guarantee* and *justification* for every political decision of the hour, since its role is simply to play their servant, not to say their maid-of-all-work. What does it matter that it produces nothing, that it is incapable of outshining its opponents? At least it serves as an *internal ideology* within the party, providing its cadres and its militants with a lexicon of common passwords, an internal system of signs of recognition which help to strengthen the unity of the organization. Now unity is not of course a bad thing – but unity for its own sake, unity for any end and *by any means?* All this is only possible at a price, of course, since the decay of philosophy into a practical ideology, sustaining the political ideology of the party by providing it with the guarantee of the 'laws' of the dialectic, encourages the party to close in on itself, to cut itself off from the outside world. It deprives it of the political benefit which a real Marxist philosophy, a 'critical and revolutionary' philosophy, could contribute both to its theory and to its historical practice, in every domain.

If we take *only* this effect into consideration (and there are more serious consequences), it becomes clear what price the French party has paid for its apology for Lysenkoism and for its silence on the political, theoretical and philosophical questions involved and at stake. For having simply passed on to 'next business', for having shrunk from the debate on the reactionary misrepresentation of Marxist philosophy, for not having turned this philosophy into a 'critical and revolutionary' weapon, it suffered the loss of many intellectuals: of all those who, for these reasons, left it, and even more of all those who afterwards never joined it. When I mention the 'intellectuals' in this connexion, I do so intentionally. They were the target in the USSR for the dominant version of dialectical materialism and for the theory of the 'two sciences': the aim was both to unite them and to subjugate them. Intellectuals – it is an effect of the existing division of labour – are particularly sensitive to theoretical and philosophical questions. They already have plenty of prejudices against the party of communism, and when the attempt is made, in the name of criticism and of revolution, to win them over to a theoretical fraud, to a philosophy which 'glorifies the existing state of affairs', then there is no need to be surprised when they keep, wherever they can (in the West, of course), their distance. Nor must you be astonished that it proves difficult even to pose (correctly), let alone to solve, the 'irritating question' of the relations between the party and the intellectuals.

Since the manner in which an error is dealt with is itself political, and in its own way the index of a political position, we are forced to conclude that whoever refuses to question the dominant version of dialectical materialism is following a line and abetting practices which have no 'need' to analyze the causes of a supposedly 'recti-fied' error. That is how Lysenko was 'rectified'. As if by accident, the dominant version of Marxist philosophy was never questioned: because its services were required.

The history of Lysenko is finished. The history of the causes of Lysenkoism continues.

One history is at an end. Is the other endless?

Translated by Grahame Lock

'The Lysenko Affair'
(1948)

It was at the end of the summer of 1948 that what has since come to be called the 'Lysenko affair' began in France. At that time the name of Academician Trofim Denisovich Lysenko was unknown outside the Soviet Union except to a few specialists in the biological sciences; few among them could have said what it was exactly that he studied.

As for Communist militants, the political conjuncture confronted them with subjects of concern on quite another scale and of quite another urgency; it is hardly surprising that they did not give undivided attention to the debates on the theory of heredity from which Lysenko had just emerged victorious at the Academy of Agricultural Sciences in Moscow.

In those dramatic days the system of the 'cold war' was coming into being, repression was being unleashed against striking miners throughout the country and inflation was plunging the working class into poverty, so all their energies went into the struggle against the power of American imperialism which, in the shape of the Marshall Plan, had set out to establish its sway over the war-ruined countries of Western Europe; they were working to assemble round them the broad grouping of 'fighters for peace' which, at Kominform initiative, was to deter the imperialist powers from any attack on the USSR and thus to dispel the threat of a new world confrontation.

On the ideological front it seemed that their tasks should be inscribed in the same perspective: to unite the widest possible spectrum of intellectuals into a front for the 'defence of the spiritual heritage of the peoples' against American imperialism and its allies in Europe, in the interests of peace. Thus on August 25th and 26th, amidst the still visible ruins of the ancient Polish city of Wroclaw, there had been a 'World Congress of Intellectuals for Peace' which, soon followed by many national congresses, had solemnly reaffirmed these objectives.

Nevertheless, in a fortnight the name and works of Lysenko quite unexpectedly became the object of one of the biggest ideological battles of the post–War period. From the ranks of biologists where it began the polemic quickly gained those of other scientific researchers; philosophers and politicians having been drawn in, it came eventually, in open contradiction to the 'Wroclaw spirit', to produce a lasting division among intellectuals of all specializations along a line which from the beginning isolated the Communists.

The article which put the spark to the powder keg appeared on August 26th in *Les Lettres françaises*. This article, signed by Jean Champenoix, made the first page, under the imposing heading 'A Great Scientific Event: Heredity is not Governed by Mysterious Factors'. It was presented as a report on the supposedly 'historic' Session of the USSR Academy of Agricultural Sciences which had just taken place in Moscow from July 31st to August 7th.

What it hailed was nothing less than the birth of a new science: an event already in itself of a kind to arouse passions and controversies, as many examples in the history of the sciences bear witness. But what astonished both Lysenko's supporters and his opponents was the fact that the new 'biology' whose birth the Soviet Academicians had just officially sanctioned deliberately set itself against a discipline – genetics – that was held to be one of the major scientific victories of the first half of the twentieth century. It dismissed as 'metaphysical' a rapidly developing science whose concepts and theories had withstood the test of several decades of experimentation, a science which could boast of the conjunction of its results and problems with those of neighbouring sciences such as cytology and micro-biology, and whose medical applications had also made Soviet laboratories like the Institute of Medical Genetics, directed by Levit, and the Institute of Experimental Biology, directed by Kol'tsov, internationally famous.

What was shocking was the fact that the article in *Les Lettres françaises* attempted to justify this counterposition of Lysenko's doctrine to 'classical' genetics by arguments which were not of a scientific nature, but ideological and political.

Indeed the author presented the Session he was reviewing as 'the outcome of a long struggle going far beyond the bounds of biological science, or even of science, and of the country in which it is taking place, which had been going on since before the War'. And so that the scope of the discussion should be perfectly clear, he went on as follows: 'As everything fits together in our world, the two hostile and irreconcilable conceptions which clashed on the apparently specialized and circumscribed terrain of biology, or more precisely of genetics, were the same as those that have confronted one another and still do confront one another through-out the modern world, in sciences, philosophy, economics, politics: the conception that makes men exterminate one another on the battlefields and sterilizes the resources of the earth and of human intelligence; the conception that wishes to unite all the citizens of the world so that they can increase and multiply, along with their fields and their flocks. Broadly, very broadly speaking, these debates have seen the defeat of the ideas that in matters of heredity, of the transmission of acquired characters, of the evolution of species, of the direction of these changes by man, constitute before and after Hitler the basis for all the doctrines of racism.'

The article went on to summarize Lysenko's basic positions and to attempt to prove their radical incompatibility with the theses ordinarily accepted in the science of heredity: 'For Lysenko and the other members of this scientific assembly who shared his opinion, the Soviet biologists who have remained prisoners of the totally idealist theories of Mendel and Morgan persist in believing that the transmission and modification of hereditary characters is achieved by means of a substance in the scholastic sense of the term, or, so to speak, a "virtue" – in the sense in which Molière's doctor claimed that opium causes sleep because it possesses dormi-tive virtue – which resides only in the chromosomes, in embryonic cells. . . . It follows from this theory that the properties acquired by the animal or plant organism during its life as a result of special circumstances, the influence of the environment, are not trans-mitted from generation to generation. . . . The grand idea defended by Lysenko is as follows: the living organism, animal or plant, is in all its parts, which reciprocally and constantly interact with one another. The organism and the conditions necessary for its life represent a unity.'

Much could be said about this passage. But all things considered, it reproduces fairly faithfully the misunderstandings and impostures on which Lysenko's report was built.

At any rate, no one could miss the seriousness of the injunction it unambiguously formulated: biologists were to support Lysenko's conceptions, his theory of heredity, or else they would *ipso facto* be joining the camp of the heirs of Nazism, the side of what were denounced at Wroclaw as the 'forces of darkness'. It was also clear that the summons was not addressed to biologists alone but to all scientists and intellectuals. Hence the bitterness and breadth of the discussion which took place in the succeeding days.

Already on September 8th, a column was opened in the paper *Combat* under the general heading 'Mendel . . . or Lysenko? Have the Sciences of Heredity been Built on an Error for Two Hundred Years?' In the presentation of its inquiry, the newspaper announced that it proposed 'to ask a number of personalities from the scientific world about the interpretations made in France of the works of the Soviet scientist Lysenko, in order to discover what differentiates his work from that of his predecessors and to what extent it has suffered from partisan distortions'. So, from September 8th to 15th, on the first page, famous scientists one after another took up positions on the basis of the still fragmentary information then available to them.

Let me run through the contributions to this debate.

After a cautious article by Jean Rostand, who reckoned that 'even if the facts announced by Lysenko are accurate as facts, it may be that they did not have the significance he attributes to them,' and consequently applied himself to negotiating the possibility of a compromise between Lysenko's interpretation and 'an interpretation different from his and still in conformity with the teachings of classical genetics,' two sharply polemical articles were to give the debate its full dimensions.

One by Maurice Daumas,[1] who first threw the name of Galileo into the controversy. After a stinging criticism of the 'supposedly scientific' content of the article in *Les Lettres françaises*, denouncing notably its obvious falsification of the theses of classical genetics, Daumas concluded that this was not indeed a matter of a scientific debate proper, analogous for example to the memorable disputes

---

[1] Maurice Daumas was at that time Assistant Curator at the Musée des Arts et Métiers.

between Cuvier and Geoffroy Saint-Hilaire or Newton and the Cartesians: 'In fact, the recent Moscow debates take us back to the epoch of Galileo. With them come the same procedures of intimidation, the same arguments (almost literally) to smear theses and individuals, the same one-sidedness, the same absolutism. . . . The great sorrow of our epoch – it can no longer be a matter of indignation – is thus that such an undertaking should be possible today. But those who have launched it with such massive publicity should remember that despite the Congregation, Copernicus' system triumphed over Ptolemy's.' Thus Galileo came to be central to the debate, and he has never left it: the geneticist Zhores Medvedev,[2] writing in the 1960's a now famous book on 'The Rise and Fall of T. D. Lysenko', was to identify Vavilov, Lysenko's opponent who died in deportation, with Galileo; as for the Communists, in the heat of battle they replied by making the opposite identification.

On September 15th the inquiry ended with an intervention by Jacques Monod[3] who asked and protested: 'How could Lysenko have obtained sufficient power and influence to subjugate his colleagues, win the support of the radio and the press, the approval of the Central Committee and of Stalin in person, to the extent that today Lysenko's derisory truth is the official truth guaranteed by the state, that everything that deviates from it is "irrevocably outlawed" from Soviet science. . . . All this is senseless, monstrous, unbelievable. Yet it is true. What has happened?'

Monod's answer to this question was not to vary. He was still repeating it in 1970 in his introduction to Medvedev's book. It is a global answer: all is explained, he wrote, by the 'mortal decay into which socialist thought has fallen in the Soviet Union. There seems no possible alternative to this conclusion, painful as it may be to anyone who has long set all his hopes on the emergence of socialism in Russia as the first stage of its triumph throughout the world.'

To these increasingly virulent attacks one single reply: that of a man divided in whose honour it must be said that he refused to

[2] Zhores Medvedev was a student of biology at the time of Lysenko's rise in the Soviet Union. Even before Lysenko's 'fall' he set out to write a book on the affair, extracts from which were passed clandestinely from hand to hand. This book came out in the USA in 1968 and was translated into French and published in an abridged edition in France by Gallimard in 1971.

[3] At that time Jacques Monod was laboratory head at the Institut Pasteur.

the end the impossible choice that so many wanted to impose on him between his political convictions and his scientific conceptions. That man: Marcel Prenant, former partisan leader, member of the Central Committee of the French Communist Party and internationally famous biologist.

In his intervention of September 14th, he marked himself off from 'enthusiasts and insufficiently experienced vulgarizers', and from 'the critics whose ill-will is expressed *a priori*', and then sought to control the conflagration by negotiating with and against everyone a point of agreement between Lysenkoism and classical genetics. 'The really new point seems to be as follows. Whereas hitherto the experimental interventions made by geneticists (by irradiation, for example) have enabled them to increase the percentage of mutations but not to produce a determinate transformation, Michurin and Lysenko say that they have, by suitable techniques such as extreme changes in temperature, obtained in certain cases the hereditary fixation of characters acquired under environmental influence and hence knowable in advance. There is nothing absurd in this. . . . It may well be that on top of that Lysenko's texts are often obscure, that he sometimes appeals in a way to which we are unaccustomed to argument by authority, quoting from Marx, Engels, Darwin, Timiryazev, but this cannot gainsay the fact that a whole people is today profiting by the work of Michurin and Lysenko. Which of our vehement critics has obtained comparable results?'

In *La Pensée* at the end of the year, Marcel Prenant took up the same arguments: the Lysenkoists had obtained good practical results in agriculture where 'classical' geneticists had been ineffective; the facts he signalled should be closely studied; no doubt they were compatible with Mendelist theory. When the review *Europe* had published the full documentation of the debate, Prenant attempted a final evasion: Lysenko's criticisms, he claimed, do not apply to genetics itself but only to the reactionary, mystical or racist, idealist exploitations to which it had been subject in Germany and the USA. . . . As for the 'positive' content of the doctrine, he asked that it be examined seriously.

Meanwhile what was already the 'Lysenko affair' had become an object of everyday political struggle: on September 5th, Charles Dumas[4] had written in *Le Populaire* a very sharp response to *Les*

---

[4] At the time Charles Dumas was head of the foreign policy department of the socialist journal.

Lettres françaises entitled 'Return to the Middle Ages'. Having recalled that all tyrannical regimes have always wanted to 'subject the arts and philosophy to the will of the holders of power', he went on to justify the title of his article: 'Where it is no longer possible to smile is when it is claimed that from now on science must submit to the doctrine of a political ideology, because it is an attempt to take the human spirit back to the worst periods of the middle ages.'

Georges Cogniot replied in *L'Humanité*, September 10th: 'Soviet Science and the Socialists of the Middle Ages'. Cogniot repeated, without an iota's change, the theses unfolded in *Les Lettres françaises*; he identified Mendelism and metaphysics and gave credence to Lysenko's hundredfold repeated declarations of his fidelity to Darwinism; he recalled the persistent hostility of reactionary ideologists to Darwin's doctrine and closed with the following counter-attack in the form of a diatribe: 'All the servants of capitalism ask of science something other than objective truth: they ask of it justification for social and philosophical systems condemned by the facts; they pursue aims foreign to the search for truth. . . . The time is not long since when the biologist Scopes was put on trial in Dayton, Tennessee, for having taught evolutionism. Ten years after the Soviet Revolution the states of Tennessee and Mississippi passed laws prohibiting the teaching of Darwinism, a law of Texas removed everything about evolution from school textbooks, no less odious "dogmatic slaveries" were instituted by the ministries of North Carolina, California, the school boards in Atlanta, capital of Georgia, and many others. There is the Inquisition, Messrs. socialists of the middle ages.'

Clearly, Marcel Prenant's critical moderation was no longer in season: he was forced into silence and then to leave the Party. There began the time of what Althusser, in the preface to *For Marx*, called 'conviction, whether inspired or forced'.

To Aragon then fell the responsibility for refuting the hostile arguments.[5] Thus: 'Without taking sides between the two tendencies, a philistine may be allowed to observe that the first decrees man's inability to change the course of species, to direct living

---

[5] To be fair, however, it should be added that some biologists subsequently helped to spread Lysenkoist theses in France. They formed a 'French Association of Friends of Michurin'. See for example the publications of Cl. Ch. Mathon, one of the leading spirits in this Association. Notably his *Études mitchouriniennes sur les céréales* (together with M. Stroun) and his article 'Quelques aspects du mitchourinisme' in the *Revue générale des sciences pures et appliquées*, nos. 3–4, 1951.

nature, while the second claims to justify man's power to change the course of species, to direct the course of species, to direct heredity. He may be allowed to say to himself that someone who does not lay claim to dialectical materialism, to Marxism, will be less embarrassed if he chooses the first theory than a Marxist who, on every occasion, not just in biology, regards it as his role not merely to explain the world but also to change it. A non-Marxist is certainly more comfortable with the first theory than a Marxist. Or, to make myself more plain, if Marxism is postulated first, before going on to biology, the Marxist biologist will certainly be prejudiced in favour of the Michurinist theory which justifies the possibility of human action on living nature.' And this conclusion, which has the merit that it puts things crudely: 'Personally, I am not a biologist. My confidence in Marxism obviously makes me wish that the Michurinists are right in this quarrel. This is not an argument for non-Marxists. And it is a fact that there are men who consider themselves Marxists and yet reckon that classical genetics is right against Michurin and Lysenko. If I do not see how they reconcile this with their Marxism, I must surely blame my inadequacy in this matter, which I do not deny, and in general my ignorance of biological science. But still, to rely on crude common sense, it seems to me that they must have some difficulties to surmount which the Michurinists do not have.'

The Party's philosophers were not slow to supplement Aragon's 'inadequacy' by adding a Marxist theoretical 'foundation' to this stand. From a tendentious interpretation of certain texts by Lenin they drew the absurd theory of the *two sciences*: the distinction between 'bourgeois science' and 'proletarian science', which of course goes beyond the case of genetics, was to become for several years the favourite weapon of Communist intellectuals in the ideological battle; mathematics, physics, chemistry, psychoanalysis . . . were to fall victim to it in the same way.

The essence of this theory was set out in a kind of manifesto published by Éditions de la Nouvelle Critique in 1950.[6]

Let me go into the logic of its argument for a moment.

---

[6] It consists of a collection of articles and lectures prefaced by Laurent Casanova, in which appear texts by Francis Cohen, Jean Toussaint Desanti, Raymond Guyot and Gérard Vassails entitled *Science bourgeoise et science prolétarienne*.

Under the title 'Science, a Historically Relative Ideology', J. T. Desanti wrote: 'That there is a bourgeois science and a fundamentally contradictory proletarian science means above all that science too is a *matter of class struggle, a party matter*.' And he asked: 'If science is the product of a class, how is one to understand the objectivity of its content? How is

First, it established that every science has a class character. Now this class character does not just affect the socio-material conditions of research, as is plain to any sociologism, but also, something much more radical, the *concepts* and *theories* that it gives rise to. If one added that by virtue of the division of manual and intellectual labour integral to the existence of class societies, it is always the mark of the ruling class that science bears, it was easy to draw the conclusion that science as it exists in the middle of the twentieth century is 99 per cent 'bourgeois science': all its productions are marked with the brand of its class of origin; they express the *interest* that this class has in knowing reality and transforming it to its advantage.

Here a question and an objection arise: this being so, what then distinguishes bourgeois 'science' from mere bourgeois ideology? Can one still say, as the Marxist classics maintained, that scientific knowledges are *objective?* How is one to explain the effective, if still imperfect, control of natural phenomena that humanity has acquired thanks to the sciences, and especially to the 'bourgeois' sciences? The answer came in two stages: if it is true, it was explained, that when the bourgeoisie was involved in the conquest of power it had an interest in knowing reality objectively and was

---

one to understand the undoubted *unity of its development?*' Answer: 'Science is the fruit of human labour and in this labour man determines nature as it is in itself. To transform the thing in itself into a thing for us means to attack brute nature with tools forged in contact with it and to learn by this labour to master it. Now, this transformation is not the work of man in isolation; it uses tools, it is achieved in labour. Hence it is the fruit of the whole society: the way it is achieved reflects the state of the productive forces that sustain the whole social edifice; and hence also the interests of the class whose social activity promotes the productive forces and sustains the form of organisation of labour. Hence the content of science must retain the dialectical unity of the two terms of this transformation: human labour on the one hand, nature on the other. This unity is precisely what Lenin calls the "thing for us", or, in other words, the sector of nature already dominated by human practice. This dialectical relation must also be found in the development of science. This development always has a social content: as such it is always relative to the state of the productive forces, always linked to class struggles (often by remote links), always expressive of the interests and consciousness of a class. But this development thereby expresses the degree of mastery and domination that a given society has achieved over nature. It thus contains and uses, even as it extends it, the sector of nature already dominated. This explains how science can be one in its development and is yet linked by a necessary bond to class struggles; this explains how the content of science can be objective and yet express the viewpoint of the rising or ruling class.'

This text is undoubtedly the most systematic justification for the philosophical basis of Lysenkoism. It has the exceptional interest that it confronts the crucial philosophical questions posed by the theory of the 'two sciences' without side-stepping: an imprudence from which the majority of Soviet philosophers were retreating at the same moment.

thus able to produce authentically scientific knowledges, on the contrary, once its struggle became a defensive one and it had to preserve its power against the proletariat, this was not allowed it as a victim of its own interest in masking reality from its opponent. Thus, where heredity is concerned: with Darwin the bourgeoisie reached the limits of the knowledges of which it was capable. What came after was no more than ideological defences that, far from developing Darwinism, have betrayed its essence.

With the crisis of capitalism has come the hour of 'proletarian science': now, by its position in the class struggle, only the proletariat can know reality objectively-scientifically, because it alone is interested in its transformation. That it should lay down the cornerstones of this science of a new type in the Soviet Union, the first country in which it is in power, is nothing if not logical. Lysenko's 'biology' was thus presented as the first achievement of this new era in the history of the sciences to which the October Revolution had given birth; the critique of 'classical' genetics as the first tremor in an earthquake which was to spread throughout the scientific edifice.

However obviously hazardous it seems today, this theoretical construction had the appearance of consistency. Reinforced by the authority of the highest scientific and political instances of the USSR, it was strong enough to spur the enthusiasm of a number of philosophers and to pitch some scientists into the most tragic of intellectual collapses.

Such were the first exchanges in the great 'quarrel' (*bagarre*), in Aragon's words, that constituted the 'Lysenko affair' in France; such, in their mutual intransigence, were the positions of the two opposed camps confronting one another after September 1948. The polemic broke out, as we have seen, vis-à-vis an article which gave a review of Lysenko's Report to the Academy of Agricultural Sciences in Moscow. It was not long before the precise contents of the Report which occasioned that article were revealed, thanks to an issue of the magazine *Europe* (Nos. 33–4, September–October 1948).

* * *

If we restrict ourselves to its title, Lysenko's Report concerns 'the situation in biological science'.[7] But this is specified in its opening

---

[7] The full proceedings of the Session were translated into English and published as *The Situation in Biological Science: Proceedings of the Lenin Academy of Agricultural Sciences of the*

lines, which explain the orientation of the text as a whole: biology is envisaged *as the foundation of scientific agronomy*. Hence the examination centres on 'the laws of the life and development of vegetable and animal forms, i.e., primarily . . . the science known for half a century now as genetics' (p. 11).

There follow the broad outlines of a history of biology which Lysenko made begin with Darwin. Not for convenience, but because in his eyes 'the appearance of Darwin's teaching, expounded in his book, *The Origin of Species*, marked the beginning of scientific biology' (ibid.).

The key notion of Darwinist theory is, according to Lysenko, the theory of natural and artificial selection by adaptation. By his theory of selection, Darwin gave a rational explanation of the *adaptation* of living nature, thus generalizing the results obtained empirically over centuries by agriculturalists and breeders. 'Agricultural practice,' explained Lysenko, 'served Darwin as the material basis for the elaboration of his theory of evolution, which explained the natural causes of the purposiveness we see in the structure of the organic world' (p. 12).

The Report went on to recall Engels's dual appreciation of Darwin's achievement:[8] on the one hand, the theory of natural selection is celebrated as one of the three essential discoveries which together with that of the cell and that of the transformation of energy, have advanced by leaps and bounds our 'knowledge of the interconnection of natural processes' (ibid.) and on the other, it is criticized for a series of mistakes, all of which in the last analysis come down to Darwin's borrowings from Malthus's reactionary teachings.

Following Engels, Lysenko cited Darwin himself: 'In October 1838, that is, fifteen months after I had begun my systematic enquiry, I happened to read for amusement *Malthus on Population*, and, being well prepared to appreciate the struggle for existence which everywhere goes on from long-continued observation of the habits of animals and plants, it at once struck me that under

---

USSR Session: July 31st–August 7th 1948, Verbatim Report, Foreign Languages Publishing House, Moscow 1949. Page references cited in the text are henceforward to this volume.

[8] The three most important of Engels's texts on the question are:
– his letter to P. L. Lavrov of November 12th–17th 1875;
– *Anti-Dühring* (Lawrence and Wishart, London 1959), pp. 97–101;
– *Dialectics of Nature* (Lawrence and Wishart, London 1940), pp. 235–6.
I shall return to these later.

these circumstances favourable variations would tend to be pre-
served, and unfavourable ones to be destroyed. . . . Here then I
had at last got a theory by which to work' (pp. 12–13).

Thus, concluded Lysenko, biologists should not be unaware of
or ignore the erroneous aspects of Darwin's teaching. On the
contrary, they should ponder Engels's words: 'The entire Darwinian teaching on the struggle for existence merely transfers from
society to the realm of living nature Hobbes' teaching on *bellum
omnium contra omnes* and the bourgeois economic teaching on
competition, along with Malthus' population theory.'[9]

Here the intention behind the history of biology as written by
the Soviet Academician is revealed: by isolating within Darwin's
teaching, at the heart of the theory which, according to him,
inaugurates biological *science*, an inner contradiction between a
materialist element (the theory of 'selection by adaptation') and a
reactionary idealist element (the notion of the 'struggle for existence'), Lysenko provided himself with a theoretical justification
for his position in the contemporary conjuncture: the contradiction
between his own teaching and existing biological science appears
as the result of the *internal* history of that science.

Inversely, that history appears as the history of the development
of the contradiction which Lysenko was the first to bring into the
open. But the style of this development as it was described subsequently deserves attention. We do not, as one might expect,
find the initial contradiction reproducing its effects within the
different works to which *The Origin of Species* opened the way,
but in what might be called a 'linear' manner, we find it generating
two 'lineages' of research: some, integrally materialist, developed
the scientific and revolutionary side of Darwinism – these are the
works of Kovalevskii, Mechnikov, Sechensv and Timiryazev, the
only 'true scientists' – the others, those of 'the overwhelming
majority of biologists', who, instead of developing Darwin's
teaching, have done everything to 'debase Darwinism, to smother
its scientific foundation' – these researches have found their 'most
glaring manifestation' in the works of A. Weismann, G. Mendel
and T. H. Morgan, 'the founders of modern reactionary genetics'
(p. 15).

The Report is thus divided into two distinct and sequential

[9] Letter to Lavrov, November 12th–17th 1875.

developments: one devoted to the 'reactionary' lineage, the other to the materialist lineage that leads to Lysenko's own doctrine.

In the 'reactionary' lineage, the first theory envisaged, the one submitted to the longest and most detailed analysis in the Report, is that of August Weismann. This theory, forgotten by most biologists today, owes this privileged treatment less to its position in the chronological sequence than to its theoretical content. Throughout his battle against the geneticists, indeed, Lysenko referred to Weismann's *Lectures on Evolutionary Theory* as the text in which the principles supposedly guiding all later constructions, often unbeknownst to them, are clearly expressed: in sum, as the philosophical archetype of Mendelist genetics.

These principles are summarized as follows: 'Weismann denied the inheritability of acquired characters and conceived the idea of a special hereditary substance "to be sought for in the nucleus". "The sought-for bearer of hereditary," he stated, "is contained in the chromosome material." The Chromosomes, he said, contain units, each of which "determines a definite part of the organism in its appearance and final form."' (p. 16). In other words, by rejecting the notion of selection by adaptation, brutally assimilated by Lysenko to the thesis of the inheritability of acquired characters, Weismann opened the way to the idealist tradition in biology which, after him, was based on the postulated existence of a special substance to which the phenomena of heredity could be imputed.

'An immortal hereditary substance,' Lysenko went on, 'independent of the qualitative features attending the development of the living body, directing the mortal body, but not produced by the latter – that is Weismann's frankly idealist, essentially mystical conception, which he disguised as "Neo-Darwinism". Weismann's conception has been fully accepted and, we might say, ·carried further by Mendelism-Morganism' (p. 17).

The identification of Mendelist genetics as a variety of Weismannism is marked in the text of the Report by the repeated use of the expression 'Weismannism-Mendelism', coined by Lysenko. It explains the style in which the principles of the Mendelist theory of heredity are presented: according to Lysenko: 'The Mendelist-Morganists contend that the chromosomes contain a special "hereditary substance" which resides in the body of the organism as though in a case and is transmitted to succeeding generations irrespective of the qualitative features of the body and its conditions of life. . . . The Mendelist-Morganists hold that the efforts of investigators to regulate the heredity of organisms by suitably changing the conditions of life of these organisms are utterly unscientific.' (p. 19).

In the discussion that followed the Report this last point was to be one of Lysenko's war-horses: there is no better illustration of the idealist character of classical genetics, he repeated, than its belief in the *fatality* of hereditary phenomena, the renunciation it implies in practice of the modification of nature to man's advantage.

Given this, it is easy, concluded Lysenko, to explain the total sterility of this 'metaphysical' and 'scholastic' doctrine, and he missed no opportunity for ironic comment on the results obtained by the geneticists: 'As the result of many years of effort, Dubinin "enriched" science with the "discovery" that during the War there occurred among the fruit-fly population of the city of Voronezh and its environs an increase in the percentage of flies with certain chromosome structures and a decrease in the percentage of flies with other chromosome structures' (p. 33).

Lysenko then went on to expound the positive content of the new 'scientific' biology: 'Michurinist' biology. The first principle of this doctrine cuts across what Lysenko regarded as the ultimate conclusion of classical genetics: '"It is possible, with man's intervention, to *force* any form of animal or plant *to change more quickly and in a direction desirable to man*. There opens before man a broad field of activity of the greatest value to him"' (p. 34). This principle implies a rejection of the thesis that leads, according to Lysenko, to the opposite conclusion: 'The Michurin teaching flatly rejects the fundamental principle of Mendelism-Morganism that heredity is completely independent of the plants' and animals' conditions of life' (p. 34). In doing which, incidentally, it is only returning to the 'materialist content' of Darwinism conveyed in the following general proposition: 'The organism and the conditions required for its life constitute a unity' (p. 35).

Hence the Lysenkoist definition of heredity: a definition presented as Darwinian: 'Heredity is the property of a living body to require determinate conditions for its life and development and to respond in a definite way to various conditions' (p. 35).

Hence also the outlines of a theory of *variation*: 'When an organism finds in its environment the conditions suitable to its heredity, its development proceeds in the same way as it proceeded in previous generations. When, however, organisms do not find the conditions they require and are forced to assimilate environmental conditions which, to some degree or other, do not accord with their nature, then the organisms or sections of their bodies become more or less different from the preceding generation. If the altered section of the body is the starting point for the new generation, the latter will, to some extent or other, differ from the preceding generations in its requirements and nature' (p. 35).

A certain number of agronomic techniques are then invoked (grafting, mentors, cross-breeding) to illustrate the validity of this thesis and this theory: these techniques are presented as *proofs* that it is possible to change, in whole or in part, the heredity of a plant or animal organism by altering the external environment. They are also given as the practical *basis* for the Lysenkoist theory.

The presumed result of this whole elaboration: a possible development of Darwinism by corrections and transformations, of which Lysenko gave only two examples in his Report. But two extremely important examples that were rapidly to become the centre of discussion. 'The time has come,' he announced first, 'to consider the question of speciation, approaching it from the angle of the transition of quantitative accumulation into qualitative distinctions' (p. 47). On this point, Lysenko did not hesitate to oppose Darwin directly: 'I think,' he wrote, 'that in posing the question in this way we may assume that what leads to the appearance of a new specific form, to the formation of a new species out of an old one, is not the accumulation of quantitative distinctions by which variations within a species are usually recognized. The quantitative accumulation of variations which lead to the leap which changes an old form of species into a new form are variations *of a different order*' (p. 47).

His second correction of Darwinism: The denial of any struggle within one and the same species. Lysenko had discussed this at length in an article published in *Literaturnaya Gazeta* in October 1947. 'At first glance,' he wrote, 'it may seem that bourgeois science, in its attempt to prove the existence of intra-specific competition, proceeds from natural selection, a correct thesis of Darwinism. After all, anybody can see that an eternal struggle between organisms is going on in nature. And organisms whose requirements coincide (for instance carnivorous animals of various species), carry on this struggle directly or indirectly, compete among themselves for the capture of food, while organisms whose requirements do not coincide (for instance, carnivorous animals and plants) wage no struggle among themselves' (T. D. Lysenko: *Agrobiology*, Foreign Languages Publishing House, Moscow 1954, pp. 511–12).

But, added Lysenko, what has been forgotten is the fact that in both cases it is a matter of animals or plants of different species. 'For instance, who can demonstrate that rabbits interfere with each other more than they are interfered with by wolves or that wolves harm each other more than they are harmed by rabbits which, having fine ears and long legs, run away from them and leave them hungry. Anyone will believe that weeds, being different in species from wheat, for instance, interfere with it and kill it. But nobody is going to believe that a thin and hence weed-choked stand of wheat fares better in the field than thick-grown and hence pure wheat. I affirm once more that no one has ever yet produced, or ever will produce, any scientific proof that competition within a species exists in nature' (ibid., p. 512).

*   *   *

These, in their brutality, are the essential theses of Lysenko's Report. They had to be summarized in order to give some notion of the ideological and 'theoretical' *fait accompli* that authoritatively confronted all geneticists and biologists, Marxists and Communists. It will have been noticed that nothing is more striking than the 'theoretical' appearance of this discourse, which argues, builds a history of biology in which to trace its pedigree, appropriates the materialist aspect of Darwin and condemns his idealistic tendencies, violently opposes its adversaries in the form of the Mendel-Weismann amalgam, proposes concepts by which to think evolution and heredity and finally takes the liberty of differentiating itself from Darwin himself in two decisive matters. But at the same time nothing is more striking in this discourse of 'scientific theory' than the disproportion between the mass of ideological and 'theoretical' arguments and the few facts invoked as proof of the theory's correctness. Nothing is more striking than the absence of an organic relationship between the 'theory' and its 'facts'. From the Report, it is impossible to avoid the impression that the 'theory' has been cut to fit the facts it invokes and that its relationship with them is one of affirmation close to injunction. This is what gives

Lysenko's Report the closure into itself which makes it quite irrefutable and implacable, once one has entered its logic (as happened to some geneticists who thought they could compromise with it) or once one is committed to accepting it. We shall have occasion to prove it: in order to criticize and at the same time understand the illusion and the imposture of the Report, it is essential to leave its closure and subject it to the facts and to history.

*   *   *

Lysenko's Report is no more than the first part of the record of a long Session: over six stormy sittings more than sixty speakers developed, illustrated and discussed each of its assertions. A discussion of the greatest interest, essential to an understanding of the Report itself, since it brought face to face in a confrontation in which neither side made any concessions the two tendencies of Mendelism and Michurinism.

All this culminated on August 7th 1948, after the sending of a letter of greetings to Stalin, with the adoption of a resolution approving Lysenko's Report and concluding in the following terms:

'This Session notes that to this day scientific research in a number of biological institutes and the teaching of genetics, plant breeding, seed cultivation, general biology and Darwinism in universities and colleges, is based on syllabuses and plans that are permeated with the ideas of Mendelism-Morganism, which is gravely prejudicial to the ideological training of our cadres. In view of this, this general meeting is of the opinion that scientific research in the field of biology must be radically reorganized and that the biological sections of the syllabuses of educational institutions must be revised.

'The purpose of this reorganization must be to help to arm scientific research workers and students with the Michurin theory. This is a necessary condition for success in the work of specialists in production and in scientific research connected with urgent problems in the field of biology. Simultaneously with the revision of syllabuses, work should be organized for the issue of high quality textbooks, and of books and pamphlets to popularize Michurin's theory. . . .

'This Session of the Academy is of the opinion that the researches conducted in the Academy's institutions should be subordinated to the task of assisting the collective farms, machine and tractor stations and state farms in their efforts to secure higher yields of agricultural crops and livestock produce' (*Verbatim Report*, op. cit., pp. 650–51).

These practical measures signalled no more nor less than the death sentence to genetics in the Soviet Union: all teaching of this discipline and all research were to be prohibited for more than fifteen years. Knowing the developments this science saw in the 1950's, knowing the extent of the applications to which it has given rise in medicine, physiology, agronomy . . ., one can imagine the disastrous consequences of these administrative measures which amazed the whole world.

Soviet geneticists on the other hand could not be surprised by the result of the Session: if they had been able to express their positions freely at it, if they had been able to defend their science, they had done so with the energy of despair, for they knew before the session began that all was already lost.

Listen to Lysenko once again:

'In the higher official scientific circles of biologists [in the USSR], too, the followers of Michurin and Vil'yams have often found themselves in the minority. They were a minority in the Lenin Academy of Agricultural Sciences too. But the situation in the Academy has now sharply changed thanks to the interest taken in it by the Party, the Government, and Comrade *Stalin* personally. A considerable number of Michurinists have been added as members and corresponding members of our Academy, and we expect that more will be added shortly, at the coming elections. This will create a new situation in the Academy and new opportunities for the further development of the Michurin teaching' (p. 30).

In other words: however 'open' the discussion, its result was never in doubt. The majority had previously been reversed in Lysenko's favour, at Party instigation. The vote for the final resolution merely sanctioned a decision taken outside the Academy of Agricultural Sciences; independently of the proceedings at the sittings that were to be held in it.

For, as the article in *Les Lettres françaises* put it, this Session marked 'the culmination of a long struggle'.

In other words, no more than the Report is the discussion that immediately followed it comprehensible by itself. To understand either, it is necessary to evoke the episodes of this 'long struggle', conducted by the Lysenkoists for thirty years. But in speaking of the 'culmination of a long struggle', the article in *Les Lettres françaises* was speaking Lysenko's own language. No one should be surprised if the real history of Lysenkoism does not coincide with the history of Lysenkoism written by Lysenko.

2

The Long Fight of Lysenkoism (1927–48)

The intellectual confusion produced outside the Soviet Union by the reading of Lysenko's Report and the violence of subsequent reactions were partly due to the suddenness of the 'discovery': from one day to the next a doctrine was presented which apparently had an already well specified field of investigations, definite concepts, a programme of experimentation and many applications. A doctrine which immediately presented itself as a constituted science, and yet one which had given no previous hint of its existence. In the mere fact of such a brutal irruption there was something unprecedented and provocative.

Lysenko was discovered on the day of his victory. But where did he come from? It was said that one 'tendency' in biology had carried the day against another. But how had this confrontation in the official framework of the Academy of Agricultural Sciences come about? When had the Lysenkoist tendency made its appearance? All questions few could have answered in 1948.

And yet, the 'historic' Session that had just ended was, in its way, the 'culmination of a long struggle'. At the moment it took up its place at the centre of the stage, Lysenkoism had twenty years of battles and many changes of fortune behind it; twenty years during which it had assumed the features now discovered in it; twenty years which had seen it undergo profound transformations and play more than one part.

Thanks to recent studies – notably Zhores Medvedev's book and the investigations of David Joravsky[1] – we are beginning to see this

[1] Zhores Medvedev's book *The Rise and Fall of T. D. Lysenko* is a polemical work. Written over a number of years, the text circulated secretly between 1961 and 1963 and helped to prepare Lysenko's 'fall'. It was later rewritten by its author and, it being impossible to publish it in the USSR, it appeared in the USA (Columbia University Press, New York

'pre-history' somewhat more clearly. We have at our disposal sufficient documentation to follow the 'careers' of Lysenko and his supporters from year to year. But it seems to me that to this day no one has successfully disentangled the real theoretical importance for the analysis of Lysenkoism of the episodes that marked this long history. For two conjoint reasons their relief has been blunted and their significance concealed from the very people who have brought them to light.

The most immediate of these reasons is the *retrospective illusion* that leads one to seek in pre-1948 Lysenkoism a prefiguration of the features it eventually took on. From the fact that in 1948 Lysenko's doctrine was consecrated as the official doctrine under pressure from the authorities, it seems justifiable to treat the earlier texts as if they were already marked '*in potentia*' with the character they ultimately acquired. This illegitimate procedure makes the history of Lysenkoism a *continuous* one, the constantly amplified effect of a *calculation* by the authorities: a deliberately engineered mystification all the cogs in which had been secretly set in motion by Stalin himself from the very beginning.

The other, much more powerful reason, inspiring and reinforcing the retrospective illusion, is obvious: the interpretation of the history of Lysenkoism to which it gives credence harmonizes with a general conception of the history of the 'Stalin period'; a conception which would see the hand of Stalin himself, or that of one of his representatives, in all the events that constitute its thread, a conception for which a phenomenon in this period has been exhaustively explained once it has been possible to find in it the direct or indirect intervention of the authorities. In the present case, it is enough to have shown how, by cunning or naivety, Lysenko became Stalin's instrument. In exchange, Stalin made sure that all obstacles were cleared from his path. . . .[2]

Experience, however, has made me realize that these presuppositions should be rejected and that, in opposition to this conception of a continuous or premeditated history, stress should be laid

---

1969). David Joravsky's *The Lysenko Affair*, written by a specialist for the Russian Research Center of Harvard University, is presented as a well documented study in 'epistemological' history. It contains a remarkable bibliography and a very accurate chronology. Its general orientation is violently anti-Marxist (Harvard University Press, Cambridge, Mass. 1970).

[2] The very expression 'Lysenko affair', often used to designate the history of Lysenkoism, is a fair reflection of the forensic tone of this idealist conception of history.

on the real and relatively aleatory distinction between three *periods* which, preceding the official consecration, took Lysenkoism, between 1927 and 1948, to its eventual form. This recognition of real distinctions not only enables one to understand the transformations of Lysenkoism in its history, it also forces one to ask what were the reasons for these transformations, in terms which cannot be reduced directly to the intervention of the authorities alone. That is why, although it relies on essentially the same documents[3] as have been used by Medvedev, Joravsky, Graham and others, to whom I gladly admit all my debt, the historical study that follows does not coincide in its outline with the one they have presented.

* * * *

The first period of Lysenkoism (1927–9) can be schematically characterized by saying: Lysenko was a practitioner of agrobiology who became famous for a number of discoveries of agricultural techniques. At this time he was only a technician without any pronounced theoretical pretensions.

It was in 1927 that Lysenko's name first came to the notice of a wide audience in the USSR, when *Pravda* published a resounding article on him.

This article ('The Fields in Winter'), which included a verbal portrait of Lysenko,[4] told of an original experiment successfully conducted to resolve difficulties in the provision of foodstuffs posed by cotton monoculture in Azerbaidzhan.[5] 'He has turned the

---

[3] It should therefore be clear that I have no intention of contributing any new facts, any 'revelations' about the 'affair'. On the contrary, I share with those who have written on the question the difficulties that stem from the small number of Soviet documents on which we are able to draw. At least I have tried to make the maximum possible use of those to which we do have access.

[4] 'If one is to judge a man by first impression, Lysenko gives one the feeling of a toothache; God give him health, he has a dejected mien. Stingy of words and insignificant of face is he; all one remembers is his sullen look creeping along the earth as if, at the very least, he were ready to do someone in. Only once did this barefoot scientist let a smile pass, and that was at mention of Poltava cherry dumplings with sugar and sour cream . . .' (cit. Medvedev, op. cit., p. 11). As is clear, if the article's writer is not sparing in his praise of the 'scientist's' researches, he does not seem to have been conquered by his personality. And no more were those who approached him subsequently.

[5] In his novel *Land in Bloom* (Stalin Prize 1949; English translation by J. Fineberg, published by the Foreign Languages Publishing House, Moscow 1951), V. Safonov summarized the problem posed in these terms:
'Here, in Gandzha, it would have been possible to grow the Southern legumes with the exotic names – mung bean and vigna, but there was a shortage of water. A fierce struggle

barren fields of the Transcaucasus green in winter,' the journalist did not hesitate to write, and concluded: 'Cattle will not perish from poor feeding, and the peasant Turk will live through the winter without troubling for tomorrow' (cit. Joravsky, op. cit., p. 58). At a time when famine threatened every year, what these lines contain was enough to arouse more than interest in what was going on on the agricultural station at Gandzha (Kirovabad) in which Lysenko worked. . . .

The experiment referred to in *Pravda* had consisted in getting herbaceous plants (peas), chosen for early ripening and planted in the autumn, to mature before the frosts. But the importance of the experiment did not so much lie in these practical results, which were far from being so spectacular as the paper proclaimed; it arose rather from the conclusion Lysenko drew from an unexpected difficulty encountered in the choice of the experimental material.

Early ripening plants were required. He therefore used a variety of peas which he had earlier worked on at the Kiev station and which he knew to be early ripening. The surprise was that these peas, early ripening at Kiev, proved slow at Gandzha! How was such a change to be explained? Lysenko carried out other experiments of the same type, which led him to a general conclusion: the most important factor in the determination of the time between the germination and the maturity of a given plant is the *temperature*.

Guided by this conclusion, he perfected the technique which was to constitute his fame, the one he always claimed as his 'discovery': the technique of 'vernalization'[6] to which his name is still attached.

The first, brief, exposition of the technical procedures this term

---

had to be fought for it. In the summer the irrigation ditches carried their rippling loads to the cotton fields; the "white gold", cotton, could not be allowed to suffer from thirst.

'There was no time for legumes.

'In the autumn, of course, and in the winter, there was plenty of water. Nay more, the harvested cotton fields no longer needed it. But what can be done in the fields in the autumn and winter?

'In Gandzha, however, these seasons are not like our Northern, frowning autumn, not like our winter. This was Azerbaidzhan, where the sun does not stint light and heat.

'Would it not be possible, therefore, to plant legumes in the autumn and winter, in the months when there is plenty of water, and let cotton have the summer?' (p. 194).

[6] The term 'vernalisation' (*yarovizatsiya*) is indisputably Lysenko's. The reality of the technique it designated initially predates Lysenko, as we shall see. It should also be noted that, later on, Lysenko used the term in a much looser sense to designate any technique which brought a thermal factor into play in what he called the training of plants.

'vernalization' designates was given by Lysenko in 1928 in an article entitled 'The Influence of Temperature on the Length of the Development Period of Plants', an article whose substance he repeated in January 1929 before the Leningrad Congress on selection and breeding.

In essence this technique consisted of maintaining at a low temperature the previously moistened seed of a winter variety of a given plant. By this means, explained Lysenko, it would be transformed into a spring plant.

In Leningrad, Lysenko had spoken amidst general indifference. But a remarkable success abruptly drew the attention of the scientific and agricultural authorities to this new technique, so that even before the end of 1929 the Ukrainian Commissariat of Agriculture had ordered experiments in vernalization on a wide scale. The success had been obtained in the Ukraine by Lysenko's father who, to deal with the famine that had been raging for two years, had sown winter wheat in the spring after having kept the seeds the whole winter in a sack under the snow. He had thus obtained a quite exceptional yield in the region of 24 quintals per hectare.

The term 'vernalization' became famous throughout the Soviet Union in a few months. Lysenko left Gandzha and was nominated to the Odessa Institute of Selection and Genetics. He published a *Bulletin of Vernalization (Byulleten' Yarovizatsii)* which guaranteed the diffusion of his research. The new technique was imposed on numerous state farms in the next five years: in 1935 2.1 million hectares were vernalized.

As is clear, Lysenko received the support of the Government from the first. It is not incorrect to say that it was this support that decided his 'career'. But it must be noted that initially this official support was only accorded to an original agronomic *technique*.

In fact, in those early years Lysenkoism was only a technique – 'vernalization' – to which other procedures of the same type were added little by little, notably the summer planting of potatoes. For example, whenever Lysenko took up the pen in his *Byulleten'* at this time, it was to give practical advice to peasants on how to use thermometers, refrigerate seeds and carry out irrigation. Nothing more.

*   *   *

After this purely 'technical' period, the technician plunged into *the theory of his technique*. This opened the second period of Lysenkoism (1929–34), the least rich in spectacular developments, entirely occupied by the elaboration of a theory directly inferred from the practice of 'vernalization' that he was perfecting at the Odessa station whose director he had become. This theory he called the theory of the 'phasic development of plants'. It was still one of the key components of Lysenkoist doctrine in 1948.

This is how Stoletov[7] summarized it for a wide readership: 'Lysenko discovered that the requirements of plants as to life conditions are not identical at different periods in their individual lives. At each phase of its development, a plant requires determinant conditions of life. Thus autumn wheat and rye require in the first phase of their development (corresponding to vernalization) fairly low temperatures ($+1°$, $+2°C$) and are indifferent to light. The phase of vernalization of different species of plants and different varieties of the same species (for example wheat) varies in length from ten or fifteen days to sixty and more. Once the phase of vernalization is terminated, the plant acquires new characteristics. Then begins the second phase of development, the "luminous" phase. At this phase autumn wheat already requires higher temperatures and a fairly long light day. If these requirements are not met, the plant does not pass through the "luminous" phase and cannot move on to the next phase of development.'

It is this knowledge of the different phases of development of plants which, according to Lysenko, allows one to *direct* this development, to direct the life of plants.

This theory was to remain rudimentary; even such a zealous propagandist as Safonov had to admit in 1949 that 'we do not yet know all the phases'. 'It is obvious that after the light phase, plants pass through other phases we do not know of.' It was to remain rather imprecise: the same Safonov wrote that 'it is doubtful whether there are many' phases, and that 'Lysenko thinks that there are no more than four or five' (op. cit., p. 206). In fact only the first was adequately delimited and studied for a small number of plant species.

Nonetheless, the theory played a decisive part in the elaboration of Lysenkoism: for it established the link between the modest agricultural recipes of Gandzha and the great polemic on genetic

[7] V. N. Stoletov, later Minister of Higher Education, wrote a theoretical and pedagogic exposition of *The Fundamentals of Michurin Biology*, translated into English and published by the Foreign Languages Publishing House, Moscow, in 1953, and into French as *Mendel ou Lyssenko? Deux voies en biologie* in the collection Études Soviétiques in 1950. Quotations here are from this edition.

theory: 'The definition of the requirements of organisms, the study of the causes of the emergence and development of these requirements, the study of the way a certain plant reacts to the action of the environment, these are the bases for the theoretical works of our sciences of heredity and its mutability,' as Stoletov could write (op. cit.).

How should one go about changing the heredity of a plant? asked Lysenko. One should go about it in such a way that the phase of vernalization begins in the *normal* conditions corresponding to the plant species considered and ends in *abnormal* conditions. To 'break' the heredity of a plant, all one need do is to play on this correspondence/non-correspondence between the plant's requirements and the constraints of the environment.

A favourite example of Lysenko's: the winter wheat Lutescens 0329. The first phase ('vernalization') lasts from fifty to fifty-five days. The plant then requires low temperatures ($+1°$, $2°C$). If the ears of Lutescens 0329 develop at the indicated temperatures for the desired time, they move on to the next phase. In the case of a normal sequence of all the phases, these ears will give seeds which will not be changed from the point of view of the characteristics of the species and will give normal winter ears. On the contrary, it is found that if the same ears are placed from the earliest hours of their growth in high thermal conditions, a temperature higher than $15°C$, they will continue to grow, but they will not go beyond the phase of vernalization and will produce neither stems nor ears: no seeds, just a bush.

It is the combination of these two processes that, according to Lysenko, enables one to change the heredity of the wheat Lutescens 0329; if, for example, it develops at normal low temperatures for the first forty-five days and is then placed in conditions of a higher temperature, the development of the plant will go on, and this time it will produce seeds.

But, said Lysenko, the plants that grow from these seeds will tend to develop *in the conditions in which the process finished*: they will no longer have the 'normal' requirements of Lutescens 0329; *they will have new requirements*, those of the conditions imposed on them at the end of the phase of vernalization. Hence Lysenko concluded that its heredity has been *destabilized* and that therefore one has a generalizable means to change and direct the heredity of plants at will.

'*Broken* heredity', '*destabilized* heredity' – these were formulae of the most famous Russian horticulturalist, the man to the formation of whose legend Lysenko was then to contribute by presenting his own works as the continuation of his: Ivan Michurin.[8]

Already in 1929, Lysenko had seized on Michurin's name. The Congress of Genetics held in that year had made it known to a large audience by the solemn homage it had paid this gardener, whose skill was respected, who was given his due in the evening of his life for having lifted agriculture from its age-old rut and who was thanked for having always loyally collaborated with the Soviet power. Lysenko was able to use this homage to his advantage: for many years Michurin had worked on the acclimatization of Southern plants in Central Russia. He had therefore insisted on the importance of the conditions of life of plants for their development: 'If you want to make use of my achievements,' he said, 'Try to use pre-prepared Michurinist species as rarely as possible. These species have been formed in the conditions of the province of

[8] Michurin's life has been told, celebrated, fictionalized a hundred times. It has even been made into a film of the same name. Hence it is rather difficult to sort out what is true from what is legendary in it. However, we do have one exceptional document which was used in the Michurin 'cult', but had not been prepared to that end: the 'Autobiographical Data' translated at the beginning of Michurin's *Selected Works* (Foreign Languages Publishing House, Moscow 1949).

It tells us that Michurin (1855–1935), the sole descendant of a noble family brought low by ruin and disease, was first a clerk in a railway office, then a watchmaker. We also know that he had made horticulture his hobby and at that time cultivated a small neglected garden rented in his home province of Tambov in Central Russia.

When he was thirty-five, Michurin decided to leave the railways and concern himself only with arboriculture. For this purpose he prepared thirty acres of land and began experimenting on hybridization and grafting. From then on his life became the story of his long vain efforts to obtain the directorship of an experimental station. Despite a telegram of congratulations sent to him by Lenin in 1922 and his participation in the first Soviet agricultural exhibition in 1923, his fame really dates from 1929. Only after 1935, the year of his death, did he become the true symbol of Soviet agriculture . . . thanks to Lysenko.

Michurin's theoretical positions have subsequently been the object of endless disputes – all the sharper in that Michurin himself was very little concerned with theory and only left a few allusive pages on the question of 'Mendelism' in his nonetheless voluminous writings. Moreover, it is striking that, going by these pages, Michurin was by no means the 'anti-Mendelist' the Lysenkoists would have him be. On the contrary, he spoke straightforwardly about 'genes' and Mendel's laws, which, it is true, he called 'pea laws' to emphasize the difficulty he had found in discovering and applying them to fruit trees.

Reading other texts – the ones reporting Michurin's 'experiments' – one rather has the feeling that what underpinned his techniques was at once an unshakable belief in men's capacities to change the nature of plants to their advantage and a 'vitalist' conception of the superabundance of living forms – which no doubt made him suspicious of Mendelist mathematics. In other words, the 'spontaneous philosophy of a gardener'.

Tamba, and it is to these conditions that they are best adapted.'

No more was necessary to Lysenko for him to use these general precepts – which were never anything but those of an experienced plant breeder – as a justification for claiming Michurin as the father of the theory of the phasic development of plants.

From a large number of methodically conducted experiments, Michurin had concluded that, thanks to hybridization, the organism was destabilized and thereby became more malleable, more sensitive to its life conditions, that, because of this sensitivity, qualities and characters often made their appearance in the hybrids which neither of the parents chosen for the cross possessed. He therefore added that, if the breeder makes sure to place the hybrid in adequate life conditions, he can eventually create the vegetable form he desires.

As he had shown, all this necessitated a profound knowledge of the conditions of development of the plants chosen for crossing and a very precise adjustment of the conditions in which the hybrid had to be 'trained' to inflect its development. Lysenko was to use these comments as anticipations of his theory of adaptive heredity.

In addition, Michurin had made hundreds of *grafts*, and as a result thought he could claim that there was definite proof of the possibility of a 'vegetative hybridization'.[9] He established, indeed, that there was a 'mutual influence between stock and scion', and that one could thus create new species.

The classic example: the hybrid of the pear and the apple called the 'reinette-bergamote'. But also citrous pears, melon-pumpkins and dozens of other hybrids. Lysenko saw this as an argument against the exclusively sexual path of inheritance postulated, according to him, by Mendelism; a new refutation of the notion of a 'hereditary substance'.

Lysenko thus turned Michurin into a quite legendary figure. Read the texts of the period – beginning with Safonov's *Land in Bloom* (op. cit.) in which Michurin is successively compared to Mayakovskii (p. 168), Darwin (p. 174), Pushkin (p. 176), Tolstoi (p. 176), Pavlov (p. 176). . . .

[9] At the end of his pamphlet, Stoletov gave a glossary which includes the term 'hybridization'. This is what he wrote: 'Hybridization: the procurement by natural or artificial means of a living organism issuing from parents of different species, breeds or varieties. *Sexual hybridization* (by fertilization) is often found in *nature*, whereas *vegetative hybridization* (by grafting) can only be *artificial*. It is called *interspecific* when the cross takes place between different species, as opposed to *intraspecific* hybridization, i.e., hybridization between varieties belonging to the same species' (op. cit.).

His achievements were qualified as 'miraculous' and his garden described in these terms: 'During all these years there had been a regular pilgrimage from all parts of the country to Michurin's wonderful orchard: thousands of scientists, agronomists and horti-culturalists, students' excursions, research workers from kolkhoz laboratories, and rank-and-file kolkhozniks. At the gates the visitors were obliged to leave their baggage of accustomed con-ceptions and traditional knowledge as one leaves one's umbrella and galoshes in the hall. It seemed as though the very power of the frowning sky and of stern winter ceased at these gates. A motley crowd of hitherto unseen plants welcomed the visitors. The branches of apple and pear trees were barely able to carry the weight of enormous fruits. The winding stems of Far Eastern Actinidia clung to poles in the ground, but here they bore large, heavy, sweet, amber-coloured berries that smelt and tasted like pineapple. Peaches fraternized with apricots. In one year almonds threw out shoots seven feet long. What looked like bunches of grapes hung from the branches of a strange tree – a blend of the sweet and sour cherry. And next to it a capricious southerner – a grape vine – waved its tendrils with their scalloped leaves in the light breeze' (ibid., pp. 156–7).[10]

Ignoring, for the moment, the accuracy or otherwise of all these 'facts', the validity of the interpretation given of them and the effectiveness of the techniques derived from them, it is clear that it was from here that Lysenko drew 'his' general definition of heredity; the one he was to counterpose to Mendelism: 'Heredity is the property of a living body to require definite conditions for its life and development and to respond in a definite way to various conditions' (*Verbatim Report*, p. 35).

This definition is not, as it might seem simply from a reading of the 1948 Report, the consequence of a deliberate, theoretically

[10] It may be asked what interest Lysenko had in thus sheltering behind the character of Michurin. No doubt one should, with Joravsky, invoke the impact of this character and his procedures on the peasant masses: in the extremely destitute state in which Russian peasants then lived, unable to deal with the waves of famine regularly sweeping the country, equipped with archaic tools, a set of very strong superstitious beliefs were traditionally linked in the countryside to all sorts of 'devices', 'recipes' or 'secrets' which smacked of magic and were supposed to have the power to increase the fertility of plants and to accelerate their growth from one day to the next.

It is very striking to note that Michurin is in fact presented more than once as the very type of one of those sages who 'understood the mute language of plants' (Safonov, op. cit., p. 157). The character Michurin has certainly 'worked' as a symbolic instrument for the mobilization of the peasant masses around Soviet power.

motivated 'return' to Lamarck:[11] nor, in these years, 1929–34, was it the result of deducing philosophically from the principles of dialectical materialism, mechanistically interpreted, a definition of living nature and its properties. On the contrary, what is striking about the Lysenkoist texts in this second period is the pragmatic character of the theoretical extrapolations their author ventured: the critique of Mendelist genetics beginning to appear in them was formulated from day to day according to – and on a level with – the agronomic experiments attempted.

★   ★   ★

As all commentators agree, 1935 marked a 'turning-point' in the history of Lysenkoism. A new period was beginning (1935–48). Not in the sense that a new 'discovery' had upset the economy of the doctrine or a new technique forced Lysenko to review or abandon any of his principles, nor in the sense that his principles might have needed to be corrected as a result of the researches which had been based on them so far, but in the sense of a general rearrangement: in the sense in which all his earlier themes, originally scattered, were suddenly reorganized and redistributed into a rigorously adjusted theoretical system. The master of ceremonies at this profound reorganization: 'dialectical materialism'.

In fact, dialectical materialism would from now on be made responsible for the *unification* of the 'Michurinist' doctrine of heredity and the *foundation* of the set of anti-Mendelist arguments that the pragmatic theorization of the vernalization experiments had gradually brought out.

An unexpected intervention, an intervention *after the event*, but one of great importance: this is what gave the 'new biology' its definitive features, beginning with its claim to be in itself a science and thus to set itself up as a rival to 'classical' genetics. At the same time, it was this intervention that fixed the Lysenkoists' objectives for the years to come: if all the points at which the Lysenkoist techniques conflicted with or challenged Mendelism could be assembled into a coherent doctrine of living nature, if the ties link-

---

[11] Lysenko's theory has often been interpreted as a 'return to Lamarck', particularly in France, because he used the expression 'inheritance of acquired characters', which Lamarck had used, too. But, as we shall see later, this is no more than a verbal coincidence, for Lysenko did not give the term '*acquired* characters' the same conceptual content as Lamarck.

ing them could in addition be installed and guaranteed by dialectical materialism, the official philosophy of the Soviet state, there would obviously no longer be any possibility of coexistence between 'classical' genetics and the new doctrine: Mendelism would have to give way both as a 'false science' and as a 'bourgeois' doctrine, opposed in its theoretical foundation to the nature of a socialist state like the Soviet Union.

From here it was only a step to treating geneticists as traitors and agents of imperialism infiltrated into the state apparatus. This step was soon taken, at a time and in a country where 'spy fever' was endemic. For the geneticists began the period of harrassment, soon to be followed by that of persecution.

So, a turning-point, occasioned if not produced by a meeting, signalled by the publication of a manifesto-article, the first text of mature Lysenkoism.

The meeting: that of Lysenko with I. I. Prezent, an Academician specializing in the methodology and pedagogy of the sciences, and a member of the Communist Party. Prezent's intervention at the 1948 session was a clear reflection of his role in the 'creative association' he had formed with Lysenko in 1935; he it was who developed the philosophical aspects of Lysenkoism; he who moved quickly on from the details of agronomic practice to lay down the perspectives and disengage the critical implications of Lysenkoist theory.

The article: 'Plant Breeding and the Theory of the Phasic Development of Plants', signed jointly by both men. Its title is an emphatic declaration of the *continuity* between this new stage of Lysenkoism and the previous works. But under the title, which is a direct extension of the articles in the *Byulleten' Iarovizatsiya*, the content is mostly novel: as in the past, classical genetics is attacked for its inability to help agriculturalists fulfil the production targets set by the Party and the Government, but for the first time this inability is attributed to the 'bourgeois character of this science's methodology'. This is how the theme of the 'two sciences' and the explanation that the theory of heredity which had been based in Darwin on the practical knowledge of breeders had forgotten its origin in Mendelist genetics, appeared in Lysenkoist texts: Mendelism was pure speculation, an academic discipline tainted with metaphysics. Inversely, Lysenkoist 'science' was presented as a direct emanation of the age-old practical wisdom of the Russian peasantry: it could boast that it was a living science linked with practice.

Up to this point the geneticists had only had to put up with skirmishes in the press and harrassment in institutions. From this day on, the Lysenkoists launched a regular offensive following a carefully considered plan of battle. A continuous offensive whose aim, declared from the outset, was the prohibition of teaching and research in genetics. As we know, this aim was attained in 1948. But it is now clear that, far from having imposed themselves or been imposed by surprise, on the basis of a pre-prepared mystification, the Lysenkoists were only able to reach their goal after ten years of merciless combat.

The first open confrontation between the two 'tendencies' constituted as such took place between December 19th and 27th 1936 at a Session of the Academy of Agricultural Sciences which in retrospect looks like a dress rehearsal for 1948.

Significantly, however, this Session had been called to attempt to reconcile the two types of research. The result was the reverse: the forces regrouped into two irredeemably opposed camps: on the one hand the majority of the directors of institutes of genetics, cytology and breeding, grouping themselves around Vavilov and the American H. J. Muller,[12] scientists of international repute; on the other, around Lysenko and Prezent, the young research workers of the Odessa institute, pupils of Michurin, and specialists in animal reproduction. The discussion was violent, the oppositions clear-cut: the Mendelist notion of heredity was already the centre of dispute.[13] As for the balance of forces, it remained very uncertain at the end of the Session.

What is certain is the fact that the Lysenkoists' attacks doubled

[12] Exceptionally for a foreigner, H. J. Muller was a member of the USSR Academy of Sciences. Out of sympathy for socialism he had gone to work in Moscow from 1933 to 1937. He was later to go to Spain to help the Republicans to organize their health service. His work on the effect of X-rays on genes won him the Nobel Prize in 1946. Violently attacked as an 'imperialist lackey' and 'bourgeois scientist', he resigned from the Soviet Academy in 1948. Loren Graham's book *Science and Philosophy in the Soviet Union* (Alfred Knopf, New York and Allen Lane, London 1972) has in an appendix a remarkable article by him (first published in 1934) which is well worth reading: 'Lenin's Doctrine in Relation to Genetics'. Graham's is one of the few well-documented books on the question which is not blinded by anti-Marxist bias.

[13] On this occasion Lysenko stated: 'We deny . . . particles, corpuscles of heredity. If a man denies the existence of "particles of temperature", denies the existence of a "specific thermal substance", does that mean he denies the existence of temperature as a property

in violence in the following months. Thus a little later, Prezent published in Lysenko's magazine a long article accusing the geneticists of being 'Trotskyite saboteurs fawning on the latest reactionary proposals of foreign scientists'. Terrible words which called openly for repression. The more so in that the article came a few days after Stalin's intervention in the Central Committee on 'Defects in Party Work and Measures for Liquidating Trotskyite and other Double-Dealers'. The magazine had, moreover, decided to reprint the text of this speech at the beginning of the number in which the geneticists were attacked in the terms given above. . . .

The appeal did not fall on deaf ears: the International Congress of Genetics planned to take place at Moscow in 1937 was postponed. Meister, Levit, Gorbunov and Muratov were arrested in 1938. Lysenko was made President of the Academy of Agricultural Sciences on February 28th 1938.

Encouraged by these first successes, Lysenko and his friends redoubled the virulence of their polemic. Their main target was now Vavilov, the most prestigious of Soviet geneticists, who had given a resolutely anti-Michurinist thrust to teaching at the Moscow Institute of Genetics of which he was still the director. Once again Prezent was in the forefront: 'Our native geneticists,' he wrote, 'those attempting to defend the "truths" of Mendelism-Morganism, should take pause over the significant fact that the philosophical foundations of the theory they defend have already found a place in the history of pseudo-science, in Dühring's pseudo-philosophy, exposed by Engels' (cit. Medvedev, op. cit., p. 55).

As for Lysenko, he was concerned to 'clean up' the Academy whose presidency he had conquered: 'It is necessary to expel from the institutes and stations the methods of bourgeois science which were cultivated in every possible way by the enemies of the people, the Trotskyite-Bukharinist diversionists who operated in the All-Union Academy of Agricultural Sciences' (cit. ibid., p. 54).

This campaign ended with the arrest of Vavilov (1940) and his death in deportation shortly thereafter.[14] However, by the out-

---

of matter? We deny the existence of corpuscles and molecules of a special "hereditary substance", but at the same time we not only recognize the existence of a hereditary nature, a hereditary basis, of plant forms, but, in our opinion, understand it far better than you geneticists do' (*Agrobiology*, op. cit., p. 188).

[14] Medvedev, who dedicates his book to him, gives an excellent portrait of N. I. Vavilov, and a moving account of the conditions of his death. Nikolai Ivanovich Vavilov was the

break of the War, the game was far from won by the Lysenkoists: their positions were still weak in the various biological research institutes, and in the educational establishments. The school books still expounded the bases of 'Mendelism-Morganism' and breathed not a word about Michurinism. The only domain which they controlled was thus still that of the institutions of education and research which depended on the Ministry of Agriculture, in which they held the key posts.

As for the Central Committee of the Party, once the four 'saboteurs' had been arrested, it remained silent, non-committal. Despite Lysenkoist pressure, it refused to take sides on the theory. This was clear in 1939 when the magazine *Pod Znamenem Marksizma (Under the Banner of Marxism)*, the organ that published official Party positions on ideological and cultural matters, organized a conference on the question of the biological sciences. It might have been expected that this meeting would sign the geneticists' death warrant. This was not the case. The philosopher Mitin, Stalin's authorized spokesman, implied unambiguously that the aim of the conference was to work out a *compromise* between the two tendencies. Mitin went so far as to qualify the Lysenkoists' intransigence as 'anti-intellectualism'. The meeting closed with a reconfirmation of the *status quo*.

But at the same time the Lysenkoists' strength in the agricultural institutions was increased by the support of the partisans of a system of *pedology* (the science of soils): the system of V. R. Vil'yams (or Williams), which in fact had no theoretical relationship with Lysenko's theory, except for its voluntarist character and the philosophical principles on which it claimed to rest. Indeed, Vil'yams claimed that, by applying dialectical materialism to the science of soils it is possible to change their nature – and thereby the climate – at will.

And he proved it methodically. This 'proof' and his practical

---

founder of the Lenin Academy of Agricultural Sciences. He long directed, as we shall see, the Institute of Genetics of the USSR Academy of Sciences and the All-Union Institute of Plant Breeding.

It is in this capacity that he was known to the whole world: from 1920, he had proposed and begun to carry out a plan for the reorganization of the plant resources of the country. His methodical investigations took him everywhere in the USSR and to many foreign countries. He was thus able to gather together more than 150,000 plant varieties and species, constituting an experimental material unique in the world. Lenin having personally encouraged Vavilov's work, he enjoyed a double prestige, scientific and political.

conclusions constituted what has been called the *grassland system* or system of 'lea rotation'. 'System' because it was from the grandiose genesis of soils that the practical agronomic methods proposed were deduced.[15]

Vil'yams established deductively that the 'golden age' of the soils is that of the chernozems, the black earths. What is the peculiar characteristic of the chernozems? They are *structured*. What is the origin of the impoverishment of the Russian steppes, so spectacular and so tragic? The progressive loss of this structure: the destructuration of the soils. Thus 'restructuration' came to be Vil'yams' slogan.

Hence the techniques deduced to reconstitute the soils. What has to be achieved, Vil'yams said, is in sum to 'return to grassland' – to return to the age of the soils' fertility. To retrace the path that has degraded turf into steppe. The solution: to plant not 'steppe plants'

[15] Vil'yams presented his *Pedology* as the 'table of the single and gigantic life of the Earth from the poles to the equator, the table of the single process of the constitution of the planet's soils'.

Here is a rapid survey of its broad outlines.

The start of this genesis: in the beginning is the Rock, the Earth's skeleton. The Wind comes and attacks it; the storms and whip it; the rain and washes it. The Rock cracks; the frosts of the winter nights only have to do their work. The Rock crumbles, collapses. 'The stony ridge of the Earth is transformed into a heap of marl. . . .'

Whenever marl appears on the surface, in the wrinkles of rock, from under shifting sands or under melting and retreating glaciers, Life starts its work in the marl: it creates soil.

The first to appear is an alga: a small, black alga – 'Dermatacaulon juvenalis'. Then come the lichens. This is the Earth's youngest soil stage: the lichenous tundra: the 'protosol'.

Centuries pass, millenium follows millenium. And gradually organic matter accumulates, immense pine forests succeed the tundra. At the foot of the trees the damp ground gathers fallen needles, dead leaves, rotting wood: a grey, heavy soil forms under the forest carpet: 'podzol'. It is a dull, lifeless soil; even air fails to penetrate it, but in its depths the bacteria are at work.

Years pass and the time-gnawed forests grow lighter: grass appears. A new period has set in: the *turf* period. This is one of the most important periods on Earth, because for the first time the soil acquires that exceptionally important property: it acquires *structure*.

The zenith of this structuration is reached with chernozems, black earths, which have an ideal crumble structure.

Through the crumbs the rain penetrates deep into the soil; no matter how much rain falls, chernozem absorbs it all. The crumbs absorb the water by capillarity when it percolates through the spaces between them, and somewhere in the depths feed the ground water – that is why the level of rivers never sinks very low. Chernozem provides plants with everything they need.

Yet a new change takes place: all the spaces between the crumbs are filled with humus. The crumbs are glued together; what is called structure disappears; the earth no longer absorbs water. The land is scarred with ravines. The meagre stock of water in the soil scarcely suffices until the middle of the summer: the *steppe* period is ushered in.

And the steppe soon gives way to the *desert*.

such as cereals, industrial plants, fodder plants and potatoes, which inevitably force on to the soil a 'steppe process', but 'meadow plants': vivaceous plants, open bushy plants and mixtures of graminaceae and legumes.

Hence the system of 'lea rotation' and the prescriptions accompanying it:

— the constitution of forest shelterbelts, the reafforestation of watersheds, ravines and sands, and the creation of green breaks around areas of water;

— the feeding of plants with organic and mineral manures;

— the selection of seeds appropriate to local conditions;

— finally, *water*: irrigation, the mobilization of moisture resources, the creation of ponds, water reservoirs. . . .

Of this system, Vil'yams had stated in 1931 that it was 'the new technical basis needed by socialist agriculture'. After 1935, his supporters' arguments were a replica in their domain of those of the Lysenkoists: their pedological doctrine was presented as the only active method that could ensure 'man's power over the land'; it was counterposed to bourgeois doctrines and methods, 'passive in the face of nature'.[16] The material junction between the two doctrines was, moreover, established just before the War, via the 'cluster planting' of forest trees proposed, as is well known, by Lysenko as a consequence of his denial of struggle within a single species. When Stalin came to work out his 'Great Plan for the Transformation of Nature' in 1949, he ordered the constitution of immense shelterbelts (Vil'yams) sown in clusters (Lysenko).

But this 'material junction' was only achieved as a result of the official recognition of the theoretical kinship of the two doctrines, approved in 1948 as twin 'applications' of dialectical materialism: to the unity between organism and environment proposed by Lysenko as the foundation for hereditary phenomena corresponded the postulated unity of organisms and soil in the process of formation and evolution of the latter in Vil'yams's system.

The final resolution of the meeting of the Presidium of the Academy of Sciences that followed the 'historic' Session in August 1948 stated: 'The eminent scientists of our country V. Dokuchaev[17] and V. R. Vil'yams have worked out a vanguard theory of the formation and development of the soil. The great Soviet scientist

[16] Typically Michurinist expressions, as we have seen.
[17] V. Dokuchaev, authentic founder of pedology, was Vil'yams' Michurin.

V. R. Vil'yams has laid the foundations of a fruitful theory concerning the unity of the organism and the soil in which its existence unfolds, has created the theory of the ceaseless elevation of the fertility of the land.'

This solidarity in triumph was, when the time was ripe, to have its pendant in failure: the misfortunes of Vil'yams's grassland system when it was generally applied were to weigh heavy on the later fate of Lysenkoism.

★   ★   ★

Thus, the history of Lysenkoism before 1948, broadly summarized above, is not so simple as is often suggested: it is not the history of a doctrine which emerged delirious and emerged constituted and whose supporters progressively conquered positions in the state apparatus, eventually becoming strong enough to eliminate their opponents and impose their charlatanism as state doctrine.

On the contrary, the different periods of this history reveal one after another a series of different *elements* which finally combine as so many *presuppositions* into the complex ideological formation that is 'Michurinist biology' as it appeared in 1948.

But the interesting thing is that the character of this sequence is not a simple development from a theoretical kernel which was well formed from the start, either: the external profile of the actual history is rather a series of more and more marked oblique shifts away from the reality of agricultural practice. From the technique of vernalization to the theory of the development of plants, from the theory of the development of plants to the critique of Mendelism, from this critique to the 'Michurinist' theory of heredity as an 'application' of dialectical materialism, the delirium was installed and consolidated at an ever increasing distance from the terrain in which Lysenko had first been successful. The alliance between the Lysenkoist theory of heredity and Vil'yams's quasi-mythical pedological theory can be regarded as the symptomatic apogee of this accelerated movement of *flight into speculation*.

To have described this movement obviously does not suffice to understand it; no more than does the registering of the different periods in this history and the identification of the elements added on in it one by one. But it is an indispensable precondition, for only on this basis can the true questions of Lysenkoism be posed.

As a first approximation these questions can be summed up in the problem of the 'logic' of these oblique shifts. Why, first, the hurry to turn Lysenko's initial techniques into prototypes proposed as models for the whole of Soviet agriculture? That it was immediately felt necessary to elaborate a general agronomic theory to account for these techniques and guide them already poses a serious 'problem'. But why be rushed into deriving from it more and more numerous and hazardous 'applications'? And why the Lysenkoists' precipitation and obstinacy in drawing from their theory the effects of a radical critique of classical genetics?

And the 'dialectical materialism' invoked after the event to justify this theory and which, after 1935, seems to have governed the movement of these applications and critiques – is the 'Lysenko affair' the sign of its 'epistemological bankruptcy' (Monod)? Finally, by what political necessity did the Soviet Party and Government, not content with having approved and imposed Lysenko's techniques for twenty years, decide to adopt his theory and his philosophical pretensions in 1948, paying for this 'recognition' the price of halting genetic research and gambling Marxist philosophy – the state philosophy – on the fate of a nonetheless bitterly controversial doctrine?

3
The Peasant Question:
Stalinist Technicism

When the 'Lysenko Affair' began outside the Soviet Union in 1948, attention was immediately concentrated on Lysenkoist *theory*. It was the radical rejection of the principles of the Mendelist theory of heredity that was striking, scandalous or embarrassing. It was the fate of research and teaching in genetics that caused disquiet, the personal and professional future of the geneticists that aroused alarm. Finally it was Lysenko's claim to base his own concepts on the essential theses of dialectical materialism that stirred the passions. In fact, as we have seen, it was biologists and philosophers who then joined in a discussion of Darwinism, Lamarckism and dialectical materialism.

And not without good reason: Lysenko's Report, presented as the 'charter' of the new science, deals essentially with the theoretical principles of the doctrine. All its argument is built on the refutation of Mendelism: heredity, adaptation, selection, competition, the nature of the gene. . . . It is more or less the basic concepts of the theory of heredity that are at the centre of the text. It is also accurate to say that this refutation is presented as the application of categories of Marxist philosophy: dialectics, contradiction, the criterion of practice . . ., the whole 'classical' vocabulary of dialectical materialism was mobilized by Lysenko to arrange and unify his arguments.

Propaganda was only to emphasize this feature.

Without escaping from this image, which was impossible for some time for lack of adequate documentation, Lysenkoism can be nothing but a matter of conceptual teratology: the pseudo-scientific outgrowth of an intrinsically corrupt philosophy, the deformed offspring of a delirious politics, the theoretical version of a monstrosity at that same moment taking other, much more sinister forms in politics.

Thus in 1970 Monod explains that 'Lysenko's own writings demonstrated without any possible hesitation for anyone with a minimum of general scientific culture that their author was not a man of science but a charlatan or a paranoiac – probably both'. A paranoiac who, taking advantage of 'ideological terrorism', was able to lead millions of people into his delirium. 'A case, truly unique in our time and almost prodigious, of collective ideological delirium.' The perversion of a regime expressing itself in, among other things, the madness of one man.

However, the history of Lysenkoism forces us to correct this 'explanation' seriously. It leads us to unearth a link which is not immediately perceivable in Lysenko's Report: the original link between his doctrine and, not Marxist philosophy but *agronomic practice*.

Theoretical delirium? Certainly. But before this delirium, whose power was multiplied tenfold by the intervention of the authorities, there was the period in which an agro-biologist called Lysenko made himself known for a number of discoveries in agricultural technique. At that time he was neither the 'theoretician' nor the 'philosopher' he later became, and not apparently delirious. Without this technical basis, without its persistence, the Lysenkoists' success would be incomprehensible. This necessary reason for the success is obviously not sufficient to explain the unprecedented forms it took. But without it the rest is incomprehensible.

Hence to have any chance of discovering 'how it was possible' one must look first to the fields, the kolkhozes and sovkhozes of the 'new socialist agriculture', the state farms and breeding stations. The first question about Lysenkoism, the decisive one for its overall interpretation, is not that of the pertinence of its criticisms of Mendelism, nor that of the correctness of the theories worked out by Lysenko, but the question of the *effectiveness* of Mendelism when applied to agriculture as compared with the 'Michurinist' techniques propagated by the Soviet Academician.

To my knowledge, historians have not seriously tried to answer this question: either they have taken the manifestly mythical character of certain of the achievements celebrated in 1948 to discredit all the techniques promoted by Lysenko, as Joravsky does; or they have felt justified in concluding from the falsity of the theory to the futility of the techniques supposedly based on it, like Medvedev.

But should one not be more prudent and scrupulous? One cannot legitimately conclude from the extravagance of a theory the ineffectivensss of the techniques of which it is a pseudo-rationalization, especially when, as in this particular case, the theory was essentially constituted after the event and stage by stage to account for pre-existing techniques and facts. There is nothing to prohibit the view that an erroneous theory can be the fallacious correlate of a technique which is nonetheless effective.[1]

Moreover, can it be correct to conclude from some aberrant cases that *all* the techniques proposed were aberrant? This move from the particular to the universal is all the less legitimate in that the techniques in question can be divided into two groups which are quite distinct chronologically: those which were set to work *before* the new 'theory' had been formulated (1929–35), and those which were presented along with them as 'applications' of that theory.

Were there really effective agricultural procedures among the Lysenkoist techniques? Why were they so and within what limits? Inversely, what were the Mendelists proposing at the same time? Could they explain the successes – and eventual failures – of the Michurinist techniques with the concepts of their science? Such are the questions *preliminary* to any understanding of one of the essential aspects of the 'Lysenko affair'.

*   *   *

It will be objected that the archives are inaccessible and that the results cannot be 'checked' (Monod).

At least we do have one exceptional document which, in its five hundred and more pages, draws up an exhaustive balance of all Lysenkoist work for twenty years. A document which into the bargain confronts those achievements point by point with those of the Mendelist geneticists. Finally a document in which each camp presents its own arguments itself and has every opportunity to dispute those of its opponent. This document is the Verbatim Record of the discussions which followed Lysenko's Report.

Now, one cannot but note that the Lysenkoists' main argument is precisely that of *effectiveness*. Our methods, they said in substance

---

[1] The history of technology teems with examples of the kind. But it is particularly plain in the case of agricultural techniques, in which theory is still often struggling to explain procedures which have certainly demonstrated their effectiveness.

to their opponents, have at least the advantage over yours that they are effective. And this constantly recurring challenge: explain to us the effectiveness of our techniques by your science. . . . But what is astonishing is the fact that in their replies the geneticists were silent on this crucial point: *they discussed neither the methods nor the facts put forward by their opponents.*

The Michurinists, aware of their advantage, drove the point home. Turbin: 'It is, therefore, no accident that the criticism we Michurinists have heard from the representatives of Mendelist-Morganist genetics has one common feature, namely, nothing is said about the facts obtained by Michurin genetics' (p. 479). And Lobanov, the chairman at the sittings: 'It is not a mere accident that advocates of the Mendel-Morgan trend prefer not to mention Michurin, minimize the great theoretical and practical significance of his works' (p. 551).

This strange silence becomes particularly significant when one notices that it is repeated at another sensitive point in the discussion. Lysenko had accused Mendelism of 'sterility' in general terms, and the 'new academicians' all echoed him in a very precise sense: they stressed the uselessness, even the harmfulness of Mendelism for the breeder's work. The question which was thus central to the debate is not that of 'natural selection' but that of the practice of artificial selection. It is from this standpoint that the bankruptcy of Mendelism was most often denounced. 'Unlike the followers of the Michurin trend,' stated Lobanov, 'the anti-Michurinists have come to this Session without any real, tangible, practical results, with mere promises of "great" discoveries to come – promises which we have heard many times before. This in itself is indisputable evidence of the fallaciousness of their theory' (p. 547).

And Krylov, director of the Dokuchaev Institute of Agriculture from the central chernozem region, admonished them in these terms: 'Would not a little more modesty be in place? It is not Lysenko, but you, that have excessive pretension to infallibility and a craving to be the foremost teacher of biologists and agronomists. But what grounds have you for this? What scientific discoveries does Soviet biology owe to you? What have you new to offer the theory and practice of agriculture?' (p. 384).

'You have not kept your promises!' was the constant cry. 'You had all the resources you needed in the 1930's and you led our selection centres to bankruptcy: maize, wheat, rye, sheep, cattle have all suffered from your methods. . . . When results have been obtained, it has in fact always been independently of Mendelist theory, by merely conforming to age-old empirical breeders' methods'.

Dolgushin: 'It must first of all be noted that the achievements of Soviet selection in the field of creating grain culture strains (and not only such strains) have not the slightest connection with the theoretical propositions of Mendelism-Morganism, as is so often asserted by the adherents of this trend in biology. Indeed, if we analyze the fundamental principles by which the vast majority of plant breeders, including those who call themselves Morganists, were guided when they bred new varieties of agricultural plants, we find that they are the same principles and methods that breeders used long before the "laws" of Mendel and even the laws of Darwin were discovered' (p. 248).

And Lobanov, who stated that 'We do not know of any results valuable from the practical standpoint which have been obtained by the formal geneticists on the basis of Mendelism-Morganism', described the Mendelist breeder as a 'treasure hunter', 'a man who passively waits for the appearance of desirable forms of plants and animals' (p. 552).

And once again, the Mendelist geneticists neither replied nor explained themselves as to their failures in selection.

As for their practical achievements, the application of their science to agriculture, they cited only one, always the same: polyploidy.[2]

But when Zhebrak, under Lysenko's interrogation, had to give figures, he was obliged to concede that this method was still in its infancy and the experiments too recent, and therefore too restricted, for the results of the latter to be significant and, above all, for the former to be able to provide new varieties of cereals to the breeding stations immediately.

Here is the exchange, which in a few words illustrates the geneticists' situation in August 1948:

'*A. R. Zhebrak*: At the present time some of the polyploid hybrids yield as much as 1500 seeds per plant and about 108 grains to a spike. The variety that we handed over to the State Cereal Variety

---

[2] A method which consists of increasing the number of chromosomes in the cell by the action of certain substances such as colchicine. This increase brings with it changes in a whole series of characters.

Trial Commission and which showed up fairly well is of a much poorer quality than our polyploid types.

'*Voice from the audience*: How many centners to a hectare does the polyploid yield?

'*A. R. Zhebrak*: I said that our polyploids have been bred only up to the fifth generation. (*Commotion in the hall*) We have 96 forms; about 50 of them are promising inasmuch as they excel our standard types.

'*S. S. Perov*: In how many years do you intend to hand them over?

'*A. R. Zhebrak*: Next year we intend to hand over to the State Cereal Variety Trial Commission the material concerning several of our types. This year we shall reproduce them' (pp. 473–4).

*   *   *

These events are now historically remote from us, and we know what striking results have been achieved by 'Mendelist' genetics; the situation of the Soviet geneticists therefore seems peculiarly tragic. For *now* we know why they could not but be silent about the Michurinist 'facts', could not but recognize their temporary impotence where selection was concerned. They were objectively caught in the trap of the development of genetics: in the historical 'squeeze' of a genetics incapable right up to the 1940's of moving on to the stage of application to the selection of plants and animals.

If you want to be convinced, look at the agronomic magazines of the period. For example, the excellent English magazine *Farmer and Stock-Breeder*, in its number of December 2nd 1947 (Vol. LXI No. 3034, p. 2741): 'We have, in this country, produced great and useful breeds of both cattle and sheep, indeed of all kinds of farm live stock. Let it be at once admitted that genetical science has played no part whatsoever in their differentiation and establishment. . . . More seriously, the science of genetics has not yet the practical achievements to its credit to afford to be dogmatic.' And in 1949, in *Europe* (no. 37, January, p. 141), Jacques Blamont's remark, vis-à-vis viniculture: 'Only a hesitant practice guides us. It must be admitted that our methods of improving the qualities of the vine have not improved in the last century: we have solved problems but without any coherent theory having enabled us to predict the results of our experiments.'

No doubt the situation was slightly different where cereals were concerned – wheat and maize notably. But even Marcel Prenant in his articles on Lysenko in *La Pensée* recognized that improvements had been nothing if not very slow where the attempt had been made to apply Mendelism, i.e., essentially in the USA.[3]

Meanwhile, genetics today can explain this ineffectiveness of Mendelism in agronomy precisely from its later developments: only with help from cytology and biochemistry could sufficient information on the structure of cells be obtained to make possible the induction of directional chromosome changes in them. In the 1930's and 1940's there was no such help. The only available experiments in this respect were Muller's on the effects of X-rays on genes (1937) and . . . colchicine.

All this in an experimental stage in research laboratories, with no possibility of a wide diffusion of the results.

Very unfortunately for Soviet genetics and Soviet agriculture, it was just at the moment when it was beginning to become operational in this domain (witness polyploidy) that genetics was condemned. . . .

A remarkable 'irony' of history, in which the 'time' of a science was 'outstripped' by the demands of ideology and politics. . . .

★   ★   ★

It remains to determine the effectiveness of the Michurinist techniques that the Lysenkoists counterposed to the practical impotence of Mendelism. Medvedev and Joravsky radically dispute it. They regard the Lysenkoists' statements as vain boasts; they maintain that their 'experiments' were fictional and their results invented. . . . They claim that the celebration of Michurinist successes was part of the scenario staged by Lysenko and had no other purpose than to give a 'technical' alibi for the theory he wished to impose.

Yet it should be noted that, looking again at the discussion that followed his Report, the vast majority of the new academicians who had just announced their faith in 'Michurinism' were by no means

---

[3] There is no history strictly speaking of the applications of genetics to agriculture. Here one can consult an excellent article by R. Mayer, 'L'Amélioration des plantes en France', which appeared in *Annales de l'amélioration des plantes* in 1962, and gives a very precise picture of the different institutions which have been successively responsible for experimentation in France. There is also a brief chronology of the subject by Kenneth J. Frey ('Plant Breeding' in *A Symposium Held at Iowa State University* 1966). Finally, a volume in the 'Que sais-je?' series published in 1975, Jean Michel Goux's *Les Applications de la génétique*, which approaches the question in its introduction, without making any allusion to the Lysenko episode, however.

fanatical ideologists or armchair theoreticians: they were the directors of some forty selection and breeding stations scattered all over the USSR, and they were expounding in a wealth of detail the results of work they had begun ten or fifteen years earlier. . . .

But let us even admit the extreme hypotheses that through careerism or lack of political courage they were all willing to participate in an operation of mystification organized in favour of the extreme centralization of the Soviet state apparatus; that, unlikely though this seems, hundreds of research workers in breeding stations and hundreds of thousands of peasants using the products and techniques propagated by those stations could have remained silent about such an imposture. . . .

Nevertheless, there remains one *fact* with which this interpretation is unable to deal, a fact inexplicable in the hypothesis of such a conspiracy of silence. This is the fact that the Mendelist geneticists who, during the 1948 Session, went with the utmost rigour into all the erroneous versions of the Mendelist theory of heredity, who unequivocally denounced the conceptual amalgams Lysenko had perpetrated in his Report, who did not miss an opportunity to point out, sometimes even with corrosive irony (Rapoport), the scientific inconsistencies of the theory counterposed to theirs . . ., *did not cast the slightest doubt on the reality of the Lysenkoist experiments*, did not in the slightest dispute their 'effectiveness'. Can one reasonably believe that they would have renounced the use of such an argument to strengthen their defences? Could they have been ignorant of the fact that their silence about the Lysenkoist achievements was in itself alone an argument that told against them in the debate? Must one assume that they had adopted an absurd system of defence and therefore stubbornly refused ever to discuss anything but the theoretical interpretation of the experiments set before them, never attacking either the reality or the effectiveness of these experiments themselves, when that was their opponents' main weapon?

Is it credible that the terror which did not prevent them from opposing all the Lysenkoist theses in theory prevented them from saying a word on the technique those theses were supposed to justify?

The seriousness of the theoretical and practical consequences of the decisions taken as a result of the Session of August 1948, the open absurdity of the Lysenkoist 'theory' of heredity have led the historians (Medvedev, Joravsky, Graham) to reject without examination all the techniques defended and applied by the Michurinists as ineffective or to ignore them as uncheckable (Monod).

This onesidedness nevertheless gets them into a number of difficulties, other than the lack of plausibility I have noted and the strangeness of the Mendelists' silence on the point.

The first of these difficulties concerns the vernalization of wheat, i.e., the essence of Lysenkoism for more than ten years and what made its fortune. There is no historian of agronomy who would deny that this technique really is effective, at least when it is applied in determinate conditions, in particular in regions with a dry climate. Medvedev and Joravsky are so aware of this that they wriggle out of the question by reasoning which is consistent with their premises but really turns back against the point of their argument. They concede that vernalization can be effective. But it is precisely not a specifically Lysenkoist or Michurinist technique since 'analogous experiments have been carried out in Russia in the middle of the last century with the same results'. And moreover 'the century-old formula for the technique . . . was given by an American, J. H. Klippart, in the annual report of the Ohio State Board of Agriculture for 1857'. Medvedev then cites Klippart: 'To convert winter wheat into spring wheat, nothing more is necessary than that the winter wheat should be allowed to germinate slightly in the fall or winter, but kept from vegetation by a low temperature or freezing, until it can be sown in the spring. This is usually done by soaking and sprouting the seed, and freezing it while in this state and keeping it frozen until the season for spring sowing has arrived.' Only, adds Medvedev, the technique was immediately forgotten, in the USA as well as in Russia. . . . (Medvedev, op. cit., p. 152).

But you cannot have it both ways: either the technique works or it does not. And if, as it seems, it does, what is the point of imaginarily stripping Lysenko of his discovery or rediscovery and his practical achievement, except to pull back together an interpretation which is crumbling in contact with the facts: the interpretation that Lysenkoism is just pure ideological delirium? If, on the contrary, one assumes for a start that Lysenko did discover, or rediscover, reactualize and systematize the application of an agronomic technique which had already proved itself, then one has a real material basis by which to explain his rise, and even to elucidate part of the riddle of his ultimate triumph.

Truly, there is nothing aberrant about the 'vernalization' described by the Lysenkoist texts of the 1930's: it is a matter of changing the 'vegetative cycle' of a plant so that it is no longer subject to the seasons. By placing the seeds in an agronomic station at a suitable temperature, by regulating the humidity, it is possible to induce disturbances that rebound on the whole development of the plant when the seeds so treated have been planted.

It will be said that this is a crude method, that however 'rationalized' the form in which it is presented, it remains empirical, that today, thanks to plant enzymology and hormonology, and notably to the discovery of the role of the 'auxines', the growth factors of the plant, we know that the mechanisms of germination and development of plants are much more complex than Lysenko realized in his theory of 'phasic development'. It will be added that these same knowledges allow us to state that the success of the vernalization technique also depended on a climatic factor which Lysenko did not perceive. All this is quite true.

But this is not the point. We cannot vault over history. The point is how to evaluate the results Lysenko managed to obtain in the 1930's and 1940's and the results he was able to counterpose to his opponents.

Now, from this point of view, is it disputable that 'vernalization' was not an imaginary but a real and even spectacular solution to a problem rendered agonizing by a succession of bad harvests?

The problem presented itself in quite simple terms: winter wheat was available; but this wheat was easily destroyed by frost if it was sown before the depths of winter and did not fructify if sown later. Thus it is clear why vernalization should have seemed a great achievement. It was indeed a great achievement since it ensured fructification while forestalling frost damage.

The same kind of comments can be made about the second great Lysenkoist technique: the summer planting of potatoes. This technique was proposed by Lysenko in 1935 to solve the problem of the cultivation of potatoes in the steppes of Southern Russia. This cultivation had long been abandoned because of the 'degeneration' of the tubers in these hot dry regions.

Joravsky, who devotes several pages to this question, waxes indignant: first, there is nothing especially Lysenkoist about this technique; it had long been practised in Oklahoma, in France and even in the Ukraine. And, he immediately adds, we know today that this degeneration is caused by a virus and that a technique of this kind could not get at the root of the trouble since it remained ignorant of its nature.

Once again, it has to be stated that, out of zeal to prove everything against Lysenko, arguments have been adduced that militate in the opposite sense. Experience proved that planting potatoes in the middle of the summer made them more resistant to the disease from which they suffered. Hence it made available a technique which allowed the alleviation of what had been a real scourge. This is the crucial point. The systematic extension of this technique by the Lysenkoists had remarkable results in the South. It enabled more than one Soviet citizen to fill his belly.

That the theoretical justification offered by Lysenko was in this case not just crude and approximate but plainly false is a very important matter, but a different one. Once again it should be noted that when it was proposed virology was still in its infancy (the first virological laboratory in the USSR dates from 1930) and that the viral cause of the infection had not yet been clearly established.

The third technique propagated by Lysenko, the most 'Michurinist', perhaps the most famous, at any rate the one discussed at greatest length during the 1948 session: *vegetative hybridization*.

The same misunderstanding recurs, already making itself felt at the 1948 discussion. Isaev, holder of the chair in the section of fruit and vegetable cultures at the Saratov agronomic institute, announced the creation by the Michurinist method of improved varieties of apple trees, very resistant to the cold. Yakovlev added: 'In the past nine or ten years, numerous experimenters working under the guidance of Academician T. D. Lysenko in various parts of the Soviet Union have done splendid work on the vegetative hybridization of annual herbaceous plants with sharply contrasting features. In these nine or ten years, the school has accumulated more data on vegetative hybridization than had been accumulated all over the world in the past 150 years' (p. 102). Here too, geneticists such as Zhebrak did not argue *about the facts*, but only disputed the interpretation: if there was hybridization it could only be sexual – without being able to provide a convincing explanation in this perspective of the influence of the scion on the stock.

Medvedev, discussing this matter, writes calmly: 'Vegetative hybridization *is the doctrine* that grafting one plant onto another, which ensures the transfer of heredity by the sap, is equivalent to sexual hybridization' (op. cit., p. 175). He concludes that it is just another imposture.

But before it became a 'doctrine', vegetative hybridization was a *technique*: it was as a technique and not as a doctrine that Michurin defended it and Lysenko applied it. That the purely 'vegetative' character of the inheritance in the sense claimed by Lysenko is very dubious, that the theory subsequently adduced was hesitant and eventually false is another matter. Michurin's apple trees certainly existed, the reinette-bergamote was not a fruit of his imagination, couchgrass–wheat was a reality. . . .

If it is added that in the end many of the Michurinist techniques, horticulturalists' recipes, were not at all original since they had their equivalents in California with Luther Burbank,[4] and even in France, at Rennes, with Lucien Daniel,[5] once again the effectiveness of these techniques is recognized *de facto*. It is a supplementary argument for the thesis I am maintaining here, which grants Lysenkoism a material basis rather than seeing in it no more than ideological fantasies.

Furthermore, by forcing the issue to this extent one is ignoring the real historical place of Michurin in the history of fructiculture and horticulture: Michurin, who first set out on the road of plant *creation*, lifted botany out of the routine imposed on it by its taxonomic traditions. He was the first to achieve the systematic hybridization of remote species.[6]

*   *   *

Vernalization, summer planting of potatoes, 'vegetative hybridization': here are three 'Michurinist-Lysenkoist' techniques whose

[4] Luther Burbank, the 'Californian wizard', was presented by the Lysenkoists as the American Michurin. A Michurin who, in the absence of a socialist regime, could not find his Lysenko. The son of a Massachussets farmer, he had become a specialist in grafting and hybridizing fruit trees. Safonov wrote: 'But his science, the wizard's new, unprecedented science, did not become "OK". Not a single professor gave it recognition. The whole of America talked about Burbank, but the "serious scientists" of America were not in the least interested either in him or in his plants' (op. cit., p. 142). Burbank died in 1926.

[5] Lucien Daniel, a teacher at Rennes, is famous above all for having opposed Viala on the technique for defeating Phylloxera. The Lysenkoists referred to his thesis on 'The Influence of the Mode of Life on the Structure of Dicotyledons' (1916) to inscribe him in the 'Michurinist' tradition. Daniel's works were included in the library of the 'Amis de Mitchourine'. Lucien Daniel died in 1940.

[6] On this point see François Dagognet who accords Michurin his due place in *Les Révolutions vertes*, Hermann, Paris 1973, pp. 130ff.

real effectiveness in agricultural practice must be recognized. Even if this effectiveness is subject to certain conditions and hence contained within determinate limits which Lysenko and his supporters neither saw nor checked; even if the reasons for this effectiveness have little to do with the ones they proposed and were so imprudent as to give the form of a 'theory'.

Now these three techniques are precisely the ones on whose success Lysenkoism depended in the ten years of its rise (1929–40); to them too must be attributed most of the facts invoked by Lysenko and his supporters in the 1948 battle against the Mendelists.

But Lysenko's arguments in 1948 were simply a systematic and amplified repetition of the themes which ensured him the support of Party and government in securing a hegemony in the institutions of agricultural research and education, in taking over the direction of state farms, model kolkhozes and sovkhozes. Is it not obvious that without these practical results Lysenkoism would never have got beyond the borders of the Gandzha district?

This dissipates some of the mystery surrounding the strong and constant support given by the authorities to Lysenko's agronomic technique, but two points remain to be cleared up, two questions which could constitute two objections to this interpretation.

In particular, how does one explain the government's *haste* to approve and have applied all the techniques proposed in the name of Lysenkoism? How does one explain this rush to *generalize* the use of these methods before serious studies had been made as to the conditions under which they are successful? In fact, no sooner had Lysenko announced a success than the press rushed to make it a model for the whole Soviet Union; immediately a technique had been recognized as effective in the Ukraine, for example, the Ministry of Agriculture imposed it throughout the country, without apparently taking any notice of the extreme climatic and pedological diversity of its different regions. Thus the vernalization of wheats was very rapidly imposed over vast cultivated areas, including the North of the country, in wet regions where it could only lead to failures. The same was true of the summer planting of potatoes.

How, too, does one explain the government's *lack of discrimination*, the way it systematically endorsed every proposal of Lysenko's? It often looks like an absolute and blind *a priori* favour. Everything was accepted and approved: the real, the hypothetical and the imaginary. From this point of view, 1948 represented a culmination: all the methods 'invented' by Lysenko over twenty years received solemn and unreserved approval. It was also a turning-point: from that day the imaginary component definitively triumphed over the real.

For there is no denying it, Lysenkoism was also, alongside the techniques I have just discussed, a summum of unprecedented agronomic aberrations such as no country in the world could afford to indulge, to this day. It was *the system of fantastic recipes proposed around 1945–8 as applications of the new 'theory' of heredity* that encouraged the most grandiose government plans and led to the most tragic agricultural disasters.

Of these fantastic recipes, the most resounding both in the hopes and dreams it aroused and in the failure to which it led was certainly the planting of winter wheat in Siberia. This is how Vysokos, director of the Siberian Scientific Research Institute of Grain Husbandry, expounded the technique in question:

'In 1942, Academician Lysenko made a momentous scientific discovery – namely that winter wheat could overwinter in the steppe part of Siberia if sown in the entirely unploughed stubble of spring crops.

'Six years of tests of sowing winter wheat in the stubble on the open steppe fields of our Institute near the city of Omsk have shown that not only varieties like Lutescens 0329, Alabasskaya, etc., with a high winter-hardiness, but also the less winter-hardy varieties of winter wheat, such as Ukrainka, Novokrymka, Erythrospermum 015, and the like, can over-winter in Siberia' (*Verbatim Report*, op. cit., p. 206).

Next came the explanation for this prowess: 'In the case of sowing in stubble the soil is compact and structural, and the freezing in the winter does not lead to the formation of numerous cracks, which is what occurs in the case of sowing on fallow. That is why the roots and the tillering nodes of winter wheat are not injured during the winter when sown in stubble. The stubble of the spring crop, in which the winter wheat is sown, excellently protects the young plants against the fierce Siberian winds and holds the snow.' And Vysokos concluded: 'We have scored against the severe Siberian climate' (ibid., p. 207).

It was a long way from these delirious speeches to reality. Witness an article appearing a few years later, in 1956, when Lysenko was still at the head of Soviet agronomy: 'It also happens that the recommendations of a leading scientist fail under actual conditions of practice, but scientific workers lack the courage to admit it . . . practice has proved that recommendations [for Lysenko's method] are completely inapplicable under the conditions of Omsk and other Western Siberian regions. Nevertheless, members of the Siberian Agricultural Research Institute in Omsk, in order to please Lysenko, and ignoring obvious facts, proved the unprovable on the plots of the institute, under hot-house conditions. . . . As a result, in the Omsk region alone, in the course of several years, tens of thousands of hectares of winter wheat were sown according to this method and failed to return even the amount of seed originally expended' (cit. Medvedev, op. cit., p. 165).

Another delirious and catastrophic example: the planting in 'clusters' of forest trees according to the method deduced from the conjuncture of Lysenko's doctrines and those of Vil'yams. This was by unanimous admission one of the reasons for the failure of the 'Great Plan for the Transformation of Nature' worked out by Stalin in 1949.

To deceptive statistics manipulated by over zealous officials, cooked balance-sheets only revealing the successes and omitting the failures, 'questionnaires' drafted so that results obtained under the impact of other factors could be attributed to the application of the given technique and uneven comparisons between the yields in some highly equipped experimental station and those of an average kolkhoz of the region, it is necessary to add the *imaginary facts* announced by Lysenko himself.

In fact, Lysenko invented a whole system of chimeras, the results of 'orientated' metamorphoses of species: he flattered himself as able to transform wheat into rye, barley into oats, cabbages into swedes, pines into firs, hazelnuts into hornbeams . . . A whole mythology to which each number of the magazine *Agrobiologiya* was soon adding its contribution. A fantastic poem in which nature, infinitely malleable, bends to the whims of the Michurinist demiurge.

Undiscerning applications of techniques the precise conditions of whose effectiveness were unknown, the invention of procedures whose failures were camouflaged for years, the celebration of invented 'facts' with more to do with literary fiction than with agricultural practice – this is the side of Lysenkoism that is most willingly remembered today, in order to condemn it. This is what is stressed in order to denounce it as 'charlatanism' pure and simple. But if this aspect was certainly there, if it was even dominant in the final years, Lysenko's work cannot be reduced to these aberrations.

Once again, this mystery cannot be dissipated unless the sequence of several stages in the history of Lysenkoism is taken seriously and it is asked under what conditions did it twice change its status.

*   *   *

What did Lysenko's techniques and recipes represent in 1929? A set of practical solutions, initially located in and restricted to certain areas of cereal cultivation, to the problems posed by a succession of bad harvests. It was as such that they were encouraged and popularized. But by no means exclusively: along with other techniques taken from the agriculture of capitalist countries. The attention paid to them was in fact part and parcel of a whole policy towards technical equipment which Stalin reiterated on many occasions.

Take for example the speech he made at a Conference of Marxist Students of the Agrarian Question on December 27th 1929: what he emphasized was the need to provide modern technical equip-ment to the peasants in the kolkhozes, so that, thanks to this equipment which their size would allow them to concentrate and use on a vast scale, they could take advantage of their investment capacity and their rational forms of labour organization to prove, Stalin claimed, 'the superiority of the kolkhozes over the individual peasant economy'.

A technique such as vernalization, which requires the construc-tion of hot-houses, complex sheds whose hygrometric levels can be checked, and needs constant supervision, was unattainable for the individual peasant; on the contrary, it could be set to work in collective farms and help to establish their 'superiority'.

Subsequent years, which saw the failure of the 'Mendelist' breeders whose mission it had been, along the same lines, to apply in the experimental stations the most highly rationalized technique for the improvement of seed, enabled Lysenko to impose his methods as the *only* effective ones in this domain. That is why Lysenkoist directors steadily replaced Vavilov's pupils.

*   *   *

After 1935 a new element made a decisive change in the status of Lysenkoism. Lysenko no longer claimed the exclusive propagation of his methods on merely factual grounds, grounds of comparative effectiveness, but also on grounds of quite another kind, grounds of a theoretical and political nature: because his techniques were the only ones that *corresponded* to the collectivist structure of socialist agriculture. A new structure of agricultural production must have a correspondingly new type of agronomy – such is one of the themes of the campaign then launched against Vavilov and his school. A theme echoed in 1948 by Vodkov, who stated: 'The collectivization of agriculture was a profound revolution, equal in consequences to the revolution in October 1917. A new, mass form of husbandry arose – kolkhozes. Such a form of husbandry had never before been witnessed in the history of agriculture. The old agricultural science that had taken shape under capitalism was unable to satisfy the requirements of the kolkhozes. It was necessary to elaborate a new theory of agronomics based on the teachings of Lenin and Stalin' (*Verbatim Report*, pp. 182–3).

This casts a first light on the remarkable logic that simultaneously governed the adventurous extension of the initial recipes, their theorization, the fantastic applications that followed, their approval by the Party and the government and their triumph in 1948.

Remember the question I posed: how is one to explain the Government's haste to approve and have applied all the techniques proposed in the name of Lysenkoism? How is one to explain the rush to generalize the use of all these methods before serious studies had been made on the conditions under which they could be successfully applied? Vodkov answered this question in his own way and can serve as our guide: 'A new, mass form of husbandry arose – kolkhozes. . . . *It was necessary to elaborate a new theory of agronomics based on the teachings of Lenin and Stalin.*'

I believe it is possible to suggest that there is a historical relationship between this requirement ('It was *necessary* to elaborate a new theory of agronomics . . .') and the role systematically accorded to Lysenkoism by the Soviet state. If this is so, then the relationship goes beyond the personality of Lysenko the individual, his immoderate taste for speculation and his ambition, just as it goes beyond the theoretical claims of a doctrine constructed at a certain moment to proclaim 'the phasic development of plants'. Whatever part Lysenko played in his own destiny, its outcome was fixed for him outside him, by the requirements of a policy that surpassed him.

This imperative ('it was *necessary* to elaborate a new theory of agronomics . . .') refers in fact to an economic situation and a political desire. It is implicit in precise historical conditions on a determinate political line.

It was no accident that Vodkov spoke of the 'revolution' of the kolkhozes. For it is indeed to the 'turn' of 1929 that one should look for a characterization of this line: to the great debate about the roads to the construction of socialism that then divided the Bolshevik Party. It is well known that the 'peasant question' was then central to the confrontation between Stalin and the representatives of the 'Right Deviation'. Of the difficult and urgent theoretical and political questions which were then settled we need only consider their main result, the result with the most serious consequences as to the organization of 'socialist agriculture': that collectivization was ultimately conceived and put into practice with notorious violence as a *technical means* whereby to increase yields, notably in cereal production.[7]

This conception and this practice went hand in hand with the notion of the *subordination* of the development of agriculture to that of heavy industry and found its clearest expression in the theory of the *tribute* that agriculture would have to pay to industry (Stalin, July 1928).

This economistic-technicist conception and practice flowed from

---

[7] In a speech made to a meeting of the electors of the Stalin District of Moscow on February 9th 1946, Stalin looked back to the policy adopted in 1928 and made the following statement about agriculture, a statement which has at least the merit of clarity:

'In order to put an end to the backwardness of our agriculture and give the country more marketable grain, more cotton, etc., it was necessary to pass from small peasant farming to large-scale farming, *because only a large farm is able to use new machinery, to take advantage of all the achievements of agronomic science and to yield more marketable produce.* There are, however, two kinds of large-scale farming – capitalist and collective. The Communist Party could not adopt the capitalist path of development of agriculture, and not as a matter of principle alone but also because it implies too prolonged a development and involves preliminary ruination of the peasants and their transformation into farm hands. Therefore, the Communist Party took the path of the collectivization of agriculture. . . . The method of collectivization proved a highly progressive method not only because it did not involve the ruination of the peasants but especially because it permitted, within a few years, the covering of the entire country with large collective farms which are able to use new machinery, take advantage of all the achievements of agronomic science and give the country greater quantities of marketable produce' (my emphasis, D.L.).

It will be noted that Stalin's 'technicism', blatant in this passage, also led him to a completely false idea of capitalist agriculture, its history and the effects of the size of farms on their yields. . . .

the analysis then made of the 'crisis' of the New Economic Policy, an 'economistic' analysis which explained everything by the co-existence of two different 'technical bases' of production: big modern industrial units on the one hand and backward agricultural petty production on the other.

Re-establish the symmetry, unite these two technical bases by suppressing agricultural petty production and constituting large collective farms in the countryside and you will have solved the problem, because you will find that 'collectivization opens up the possibility of a limitless development of the productive forces in the countryside' (Stalin). The problem of the 'tribute' will also be solved at the same time: the market for foodstuffs will be stabilized and the development of heavy industry, the crucial priority, will be guaranteed.

*   *   *

But this is not all: in the background of this analysis and the con-crete measures that followed from it, there is an economistic assumption, shared, their circumstantial opposition notwithstand-ing, by the supporters of both of the two 'lines' then represented within the Party – Stalin's and Bukharin's: the development of the productive forces itself would transform the 'mentality' of the peasants who would be brought closer to the working class by it; and thus a technological revolution linked to collectivization would be the beginning of a final solution to the crucial political question of the unity of peasants and workers. . . .

Stalin stated: 'The reconstruction of agriculture on a new *technological basis* produces a revolution in the peasants' minds and helps them to get rid of their conservatism and routine. . . .' Charles Bettelheim very correctly comments: 'What acts here is technology and the peasant is what this action is carried out *on*.'

Having failed to analyse promptly the reasons for the aggrava-tion of the agricultural crisis at the end of the NEP, the reasons for the fall in productivity organically linked to a slow-down in the delivery of grain, having failed to inquire promptly into the undoubtedly social and political causes that had induced the slow-down, i.e., had distanced the mass of middle peasants, arbitrarily assimilated to the kulaks and treated as such, from the Soviet power, Stalinist politics was finally driven into an authoritarian 'choice' which reduced politics to a tragic caricature. It carried out the collectivization of the land by force and at the same time made the enormous short-circuit of relying on a 'technological' revolution to produce an ideological revolution. On the one hand technology, on the other ideology: this duo from which real politics has been expelled stands in derisorily for a politics which is no more than violence and repression.

But did this 'line' at least have the expected effects on agricultural production? The facts soon had to be accepted: the yields which aroused all these expectations, far from rising in proportion to the extension of the kolkhoz system, were found to have stagnated or even declined. The result was a real theoretical dead-end: after 'dekulakization' these bad results could no longer be imputed to a kulak 'plot'. Logically, indeed, Stalin's speech introducing the draft of the 1936 Constitution stated that 'the dividing-lines between the working class and the peasantry, and between these classes and the intelligentsia are being obliterated and . . . the old class exclusiveness is disappearing', that 'the distance between these social groups is steadily diminishing', that 'the economic contradictions between these social groups are declining' and that 'the political contradictions between them are also declining and being obliterated' (*Problems of Leninism*, Foreign Languages Publishing House, Moscow 1947, p. 546).

With such an analysis of the situation it was no longer possible to think new difficulties in agricultural production in political or economic terms: they could only be conceived in 'technical' terms. Thus the series of bad harvests from 1931–4, particularly in cereals, was perceived – and thought – as the consequence of a new technological inadequacy, the last remaining, between the new base – collective farms – and the 'techniques' employed, which had been taken from capitalist countries. The agricultural revolution achieved *in potentia* by collectivization presupposed for its realization *in actu* a revolution in agricultural science. Hence the imperative: '*to elaborate a new theory of agronomics.* . . .'

Now it so happened that Lysenkoism, because of the limited but real successes it had just achieved, because of the *immediate* solution it claimed to provide for the problem of grain selection that the 'Mendelist' breeders had been unable to resolve, was in a position to claim (and to appear) to be becoming this new technique. It is no accident that it was in 1935 that Lysenko, with Prezent's assistance, worked out a general agronomic theory capable of fulfilling the expectations of the political authorities.

This was perhaps the ultimate hidden motor of Lysenkoism, what gave it its strength and guaranteed its support: it had appeared at the right moment in response to a problem and a demand produced by a 'technicist' economic conception and practice of the construction of socialism.

This conception implied the notion that technology is omnipotent, and Lysenko offered it an agronomic theory which justified the claims to omnipotence of his own techniques, a theory which responded to the thesis of the omnipotence of technology by outlining an omnipotent agricultural technique.

It goes without saying that once it was caught in the wheels of this historical conjuncture with the Soviet authorities expecting a demonstration of its technical capacity, Lysenkoism could only fulfill the expectations it had aroused by multiplying and eventually inventing proofs of its effectiveness. Now burdened with a general agronomic theory quite out of proportion to its original effective techniques, it was supposed to be able to solve all the problems and answer all the questions posed by agriculture one by one. . . . Thus dragged into the hyperbolae of Stalin's politics, Lysenkoism was forced in its turn into a hyperbolic practice of imaginary successes. This very quickly gave rise to the adventurous extrapolations, abusive technical extensions and, in the last analysis, agronomic fantasies and frauds.

This implacable process had very little to do with Lysenko's supposed paranoia, nor even with Stalin's simple capriciousness. It is the process itself which was delirious. And insofar as it was politically induced and publicly endorsed, the Lysenkoist 'delirium' was rather, as a historical phenomenon considered in the broadest sense, the imaginary consequence of, and hence the imaginary solution to, a real but falsely posed political problem. A problem confronted in terms that could not fail to produce, among other tragic effects to which millions of peasants fell victim, the 'Lysenko consequence'.

★   ★   ★

But Lysenkoism did not just play the part of a largely imaginary 'technical' solution to the USSR's agricultural problems. As an imaginary formation it also took on an important ideological function in the social formation of the 1940's, thus discovering in its duplication of function and in this transposition reasons why it should persist.

During the 1948 Session it was Kislovkii who stated: 'Wherein lies the strength of T. D. Lysenko? In that he has become *the ideological leader* of the workers in socialist agriculture' (*Verbatim Report*, p. 522). And the 'new academicians' all echoed him, adding that Michurinist theory was the theory needed by our best practitioners, the 'shock workers of the collective farms' (Mikhalevich, p. 418); only Michurinism could produce 'faith in the possibility of communism' (Dmitriev, p. 309).

All these are ritual formulas, stereotyped responses in the official rhetoric. No doubt. But it would be wrong to treat them as meaningless. On the contrary, they are highly significant insofar as they translate into propaganda terms a *fact* which is of supreme importance for the interpretation of Lysenkoism, i.e., the fact that it was the ideological cement for the 'most advanced' elements of socialist agriculture. One term should hold our attention here: that of 'Stakhanovites', a term constantly used to designate the Lysenkoists in 1948.

Stakhanovites? Initially these were workers who, like the miner Stakhanov, surpassed production norms and helped improve technique in heavy industry: but they were soon also workers who had gained the privileges of a wage considerably higher than the average, technical training and the functions of experts in the organization of production.

To describe the Lysenkoists as 'agricultural Stakhanovites' thus had a precise meaning: it designated a very special social stratum, that of *cadres of agricultural production in state farms, breeding stations and model kolkhozes*. To say that Lysenko was their ideological leader was to say that Lysenkoist theory represented the systematic form of the ideology of this social stratum.

The archives which would reveal what posts were occupied by the Lysenkoists have not yet been opened, but work such as Joravsky's has already established that these new cadres had managed to conquer the key positions in the Ministry of Agriculture. Moreover, it is enough to read the interventions of 1948 to be convinced of this interpretation. Pukhal'skii, the Minister of Agriculture, stated that the Lysenkoists' essential task was to form 'vernalization experts . . . among collective farmers' (p. 291); and Lobanov praised Lysenko in these terms: 'We in the Ministry know more than anyone else what great help Academician Lysenko renders the practical workers, how he organizes their forces for the speedy application of the achievements of advanced science' (p. 552).

It is clear that this stratum of administrators, experts and technicians could have represented a sufficient social and ideological power to give Lysenkoism, on which their careers depended, an appearance of truth, and historical persistence.

Lysenko seems to have understood very well the advantages he could draw from such a situation by organizing 'surveys' as to the effectiveness of his techniques via *questionnaires* addressed directly to these very production experts, who did everything to conceal failures wherever they had occurred. These questionnaires obtained the expected answers and thus closed the circle of an ideology which was 'verified' while itself cementing the agreement of the social stratum that profited by it.

This ensemble was not just the fruit of terror and corruption as Joravsky thinks, for example: it was the product of a determinate *political line* which, having posed the peasant question in unilaterally 'technical' terms, had as a result encouraged a new type of social differentiation in the countryside between the 'ordinary' kolkhozniks and the experts and technicians whose ideology crystallized around two successive slogans of Stalin's: 'technique decides everything', and then 'cadres decide everything'. The 'agricultural' form of this ideology was 'Lysenkoism'.

4

The Theory of Heredity:
Biological Finalism

1948 marked the defeat of the 'Mendelist' geneticists. But they were not just denounced for the ineffectiveness of the selection techniques they had sponsored; the Lysenkoist criticism did not only attack the 'sterility' of Mendelism in practice, it radically challenged the basic concepts of the theory: it denied them any scientific validity. Mendelist theory is nothing but metaphysics and scholasticism, said Lysenko. The laboratory research conducted on these lines is just a waste of time and energy, money thrown out of the window. Hence the ironic asides ponderously echoed by his disciples in the discussion: maybe a capitalist country can afford to invest in minute research into the eye colour of flies – such aberrations are what it has to pay for the contradictions gnawing at its vitals – but a socialist country!

As we know, the final resolution was to ratify these assessments: all research into genetics was long to be officially banned.

To the 'formalism' of Mendelist theory Lysenko counterposed a new theory to explain hereditary phenomena. A theory built on the basis of the *silences* of Mendelism, interpreted not as results of its incompleteness, but as so many confessions of conceptual impotence, *symptoms* of a fundamental theoretical weakness rooted in the very principles of the doctrine. This peremptory position was, as can be imagined, not without its influence on Lysenko's representation of Mendelism.

His Report and the interventions that followed built up a remarkable image of Mendelist work: a caricature whose pronounced features were formed from an interpretation of its lacunae. All Lysenko's 'arguments' were aimed at the composition of this falsified image. It is clear that they never touch Mendelism itself. But it is also plain why the debate between Lysenkoists and

Mendelists was only a dialogue of the deaf so far as theory is concerned: the former attributed to the latter theses they had never held; the latter replied in the name of a theory their opponents deliberately 'ignored'. . . .

★　　　★　　　★

I shall not retrace here the history of Mendel's discovery or that of the 'rediscovery' of his work at the beginning of this century,[1] or summarize his researches and their results; sufficient light will be cast on the extraordinary misunderstanding clouding the 1948 discussion if I emphasize the revolutionary innovation made in the Memoir Mendel presented in 1865.

Indeed, Mendel revolutionized the terms in which vain attempts had been made to solve the riddle of heredity for centuries. He rejected the theoretical schema which Darwin was still using at the same period to explain the hereditary process: when, once he had established that 'natural selection' operates as a 'sieve' for appearances of directly hereditary individual variations, he had needed to explain *the mechanism of the appearance and transmission* of these variations.

This theoretical schema, which was established in the eighteenth

---

[1] As is well known, in 1865 Gregor Mendel, a monk in the monastery of Brünn, had presented to the town's Natural History Society a Memoir assessing the results of experiments on the hybridization of sweet peas which he had begun in 1856. This Memoir – *Versuche über Pflanzen-Hybriden* – set out what later came to be called 'Mendel's Laws', the principles of a scientific theory of heredity. As is also well known, this memoir was read amid general indifference. Here is François Jacob's description of the session: 'When Mendel read his first communication to the local society of natural sciences one evening in February 1865, there were about forty people in the Realschule in Brno. They included naturalists, astronomers, physicists and chemists – in other words, a knowledgeable audience. Mendel spoke for an hour about the hybridization of peas. His audience felt kindly towards the lecturer himself. Although surprised that arithmetic and calculation of probabilities entered into the question of heredity, they listened patiently and applauded politely. When Mendel had finished his report, everyone went home without expressing the slightest curiosity. . . . When Mendel died a few years later, he was honoured for his social functions but ignored as a scientist' (*The Logic of Living Systems, A History of Heredity*, translated by Betty E. Spillman, Allen Lane, London 1974, p. 208). Only in 1900 did the Dutch botanist Hugo de Vries, then the German Correns and the Viennese Tschermak establish independently of one another and in ignorance of Mendel's work a 'law of segregation' of characters in heredity which was soon discovered to have been already formulated more than thirty years earlier by the Czech monk. In 1900 Mendel made his posthumous entry into the history of the sciences. On the 'epistemological' questions raised by this 'rediscovery' see Georges Canguilhem's intervention at the 22nd International Congress on the History of the Sciences, held at Moscow in 1971, *Sur l'histoire des sciences de la vie depuis Darwin*: an unequalled paper.

century and can be called the myth of *fusion-heredity*, consisted of
the hypothesis that each fragment of the living body produced
during its growth a tiny germ of itself which then lodged in the
germ cells in order to reproduce that fragment in the next generation. From all parts of each parent's body emissaries were thus
supposed to come to influence the body of the child, 'like stones in
a mosaic' (François Jacob, ibid., p. 207).

This 'theory', which could explain both the possibility of the
appearance of spontaneous variations without any influence from
external factors and that of variations due to acquired characters,
was called the 'hypothesis of *pangenesis*' by Darwin. He openly
admitted that he had inherited it from tradition: 'Buffon . . . supposed that organic molecules exist in the food consumed by every
living creature; and that these molecules are analogous in nature
with the various organs by which they are absorbed. When the
organs thus become fully developed, the molecules being no longer
required collect and form buds or the sexual elements. If Buffon
had assumed that his organic molecules had been formed by each
separate unit throughout the body, his view and mine would have
been closely similar.'[2]

It was the very principle of such explanations that Mendel dismissed. A real break which was made by bringing out at that time
the unsuspected link between the solution to the riddle of heredity

[2] Charles Darwin: *The Variation of Plants and Animals under Domestication*, London 1868,
Vol. II, p. 375n. Darwin's essential discussion of this question is to be found in the same
work: 'It is almost universally admitted that cells, or the units of the body, propagate
themselves by self-division or proliferation, retaining the same nature, and ultimately
becoming converted into the various tissues and substances of the body. But besides this
means of increase I assume that cells, before their conversion into completely passive or
"formed material", throw off minute granules or atoms, which circulate freely throughout
the system, and when supplied with proper nutriment multiply by self-division, subsequently becoming developed into cells like those from which they were derived. These
granules for the sake of distinctness may be called cell-granules, or, as the cellular theory is
not fully established, simply gemmules. They are supposed to be transmitted from the
parents to the offspring, and are generally developed in the generation which immediately
succeeds, but are often transmitted in a dormant state during many generations and are
then developed. . . . Gemmules are supposed to be thrown off by every cell or unit, not
only during the adult state, but during all the stages of development. Lastly, I assume that
the gemmules in their dormant state have a mutual affinity for each other, leading to their
aggregation either into buds or into the sexual elements. Hence, speaking strictly, it is not
the reproductive elements, nor the buds, which generate new organisms, but the cells
themselves throughout the body. These assumptions constitute the provisional hypothesis
which I have called Pangenesis' (ibid., Vol. II, p. 374).

and the problems of hybridization – by asking unprecedented
questions about the process of plant hybridization.[3]

Before him 'hybridologists' had been concerned to establish what
Jacques Piquemal rightly calls 'the relation between the species':
by crossing them, it was thought, one had a privileged method by
which their distance from one another and their relative powers
could be evaluated, and one could eventually discover if it would be
possible to produce a new form. Hence in successive generations of
hybrids attention was paid above all to the *constancy* of a given type.
Naudin,[4] often incorrectly presented as a 'precursor' of Mendel's,
had certainly noted that, in the first generation of hybrids (called
F1 today), an intermediate type appeared, in between the two
forms from which it came, but that subsequent generations manifested an 'extreme confusion' of characters. However, what
interested him in this sequence was that he had established that the
'type' which appeared in the F1 was really only the *illusion of a*
type since it was dislocated in the next generation and then definitively disappeared in the 'confusion' of characters; he was also
interested in establishing for each hybridization the speed with
which *the type of the parent forms reappeared* in the descendants.

Mendel too was interested in the first generation of hybrids. But
in a quite different sense: in order to study what had made Naudin
call it 'intermediate', in between the two parent forms. He noticed
that the hybrid is sometimes 'more like one of the species in some
parts, and the other in others'. Hence the idea of 'segregating'
within the hybrid the *characters* of different provenance whose
combination gives the global and approximate picture of an 'intermediate' form. Hence too the idea that there are 'dominant' and

[3] On this point I refer to the text of a lecture given at the Palais de la Découverte by
Jacques Piquemal in 1965 under the title 'Aspects de la pensée de Mendel'. François Jacob
sees three novel elements in Mendel's work: 'the way of envisaging experiments and
choosing appropriate material; the introduction of discontinuity and the use of large
populations, which meant that results could be expressed numerically and treated
mathematically; the use of a simple symbolism, which permitted a continuous interchange
between experiment and theory' (op. cit., p. 203). These novel elements are indisputable,
and Jacob's demonstration is irrefutable, especially about the break between Mendel and
his supposed precursors (Maupertius, Buffon, Naudin). But it seems to me that these novel
elements are no more than the small change of *the* radical novelty on which Piquemal
focusses all his attention: the change of *problematic* achieved by Mendel.

[4] Charles Naudin (1815–99) carried out many hybridization experiments in the Paris
Jardin des Plantes.

'recessive' characteristics. Similarly, the series of generations of hybrids that Naudin and his predecessors had reduced to the obscurity of an 'extreme confusion of forms' until one of the primitive types reappeared, was carefully studied by Mendel in order to follow the distribution of the *characters* thus *segregated*. It seemed to him that this distribution should be handled by statistical *calculation*.

Hence the three 'principles' stated by Mendel in his Memoir: that characters are independent of one another in their transmission; that male and female are equivalent in hybridization and equally determine every character; that in the sexual cells the two components of male and female origin are segregated and that in fertilization the components of either origin are united *at random* for each character.

This was undoubtedly to institute a new problematic replacing the circle of questions traditionally asked about heredity; it was to set research on new roads. Indeed, to abandon the idea implicit in the myth of 'fusion' that the theory of the mechanisms of heredity is by rights a part of embryogeny was to break decisively with a notion heavy with a whole theological and philosophical past, the notion that the species is a reality transcending the individual. . . .

This dual break opened up a completely new field of problems for scientific investigation. In particular, the *cellular* structure of heredity, postulated but not explained by Mendel, suggested that cytology might one day attain and determine the material agents of the transmission of characters.

And even before the end of the century, before Mendel's principles had been 'rediscovered' and his Memoir exhumed, hence before Mendelism had made its 'official' – and real – entry into the history of the sciences, the investigation of cell structure had profited by 'by-products' of the development of the chemistry of dye-stuffs[5] and advances in optical technology:[6] it had been possible to

[5] Canguilhem has made this point on several occasions. Thus, at the Moscow Congress: 'When, around 1930, it was confirmed that DNA and RNA were characteristic of chromosome and cytoplasm respectively, it had long been forgotten that, in giving the name chromosome to the nuclear formation he had observed in 1880, Flemming was recognizing the debt that cytology owed to staining techniques. Without aniline-based synthetic stains, there would have been no object to christen according to its affinity for a stain.' This is certainly a 'by-product': research into synthetic dyes was obviously not intended to be used in cytology. It was a response to the requirements of industry.

[6] François Jacob has shown how the history of contemporary genetics has depended on improvements in the microscope.

identify in the nucleus of the cell certain filaments ('chromosomes') made easily observable by their constancy in number and form.

Attention to phenomena such as meiosis[7] has made it possible to identify and localize in the chromosome the material support for heredity: what Mendel still abstractly called the 'factors' responsible for the 'characters' whose segregations and descent lines he had studied and which were now called 'genes' (Johannsen). Thus it was known that the characters only 'translated' the hidden presence of particles or units independent of one another, and that it was thus appropriate to distinguish between what are therefore called the 'phenotype', the arrangement of characters as they appear, and the 'genotype', the grouping of the 'genes' that determine this arrangement.

The work of T. H. Morgan, the 'inventor' of Drosophila (the fruit or vinegar fly) as an experimental material,[8] made it possible to specify the 'chromosomal' mechanism at work in genetic transmission and confirmed experimentally de Vries's suggestion that variations in characters do not come about through a series of imperceptible modifications but by sudden changes.[9] 'Species,' wrote de Vries, 'do not change gradually, but remain unaltered through all succeeding generations. Suddenly they produce new forms which differ sharply from their parents and which are immediately as perfect, as constant, as well defined and as pure as can be expected from a given species.'

Schematic and incomplete as these few indications are, they let us understand 'the progressive and co-ordinated conjunction of

[7] Meiosis is the name for the reduction division of the chromosomes during fertilization. During this process the number of chromosomes is divided by two. This reduction by half compensates for the doubling of the number of chromosomes as a result of the fertilization of the ovum by the sperm.

[8] The choice of material is of crucial importance in genetics. What was required was an organism capable of being raised in a laboratory, large populations of which could be handled in a small space, with a rapid rate of reproduction, easily observable characters and a small number of chromosomes. Drosophila (the fruit or vinegar fly) answered to all these specifications. It rapidly imposed itself as the ideal experimental material. It is plain how ridiculous was the sarcasm of the Lysenkoists who saw the attention the geneticists paid to flies as a proof of their contempt for practice. . . .

Thomas Hunt Morgan received the Nobel Prize in 1933 for having directly established experimentally the location of Mendelist units in chromosomes, thanks to his studies of Drosophila. See especially *The Physical Basis of Heredity*, London 1919, and, in French, presented by Jean Rostand, *Embryologie et Génétique*. Paris 1936.

[9] De Vries's investigations were essentially devoted to a plant indigenous to America, the evening primrose, *Oenothera lamarckiana*. According to de Vries, a new species is born all at once, with all its characters, without going through intermediate forms. A rare event that came to be called a 'mutation'.

the results of several biological disciplines with those of formal genetics' (Canguilhem) from which stemmed the geneticists' knowledge in the 1940's. They bring out all the meaning of the intervention of Marcel Prenant who wrote, in the heat of the Lysenko affair: 'The chromosomes are indubitable realities which anyone can see under the microscope, and even in a living state in the cinema. Genes are realities, too, and if abstract and idealist definitions of them have sometimes been given, others can be which are perfectly concrete and experimental, such as this: in a given region of the chromosome the gene is the smallest fraction that is ever found in isolation during a genetic experiment. Certainly an isolated gene has never been seen, but its existence has been deduced from its consequences, just as happens with other realities, such as atoms, the earth's rotation, atmospheric pressure, weight, electricity, energy, etc.'

Meanwhile, in 1946 H. J. Muller had received the Nobel Prize for a series of experiments already carried out in 1937 which gave additional sanction to the Morganist theory since they showed that it was possible to favour mutations and increase their frequency by exposing the sperm of Drosophila to X-rays.

Indisputably, many phenomena of heredity were still unexplained in the 1940's: the complexity of the processes of grafts and hybridization of fruit trees still defied 'Mendelist' explanation: it is also true, as we have seen, that the application of the theory to selection technique was then still in its earliest infancy. But this does not alter the fact that at that time the Mendelist theory was by no means, as Lysenko claimed, an abstract and formal speculation which, feebly propped up by principles still tainted with metaphysics, was undergoing a 'crisis' of growth. It had for several years been a coherent and tested scientific theory, giving rise to precise experimental tasks in which all geneticists – including Soviet ones – were taking an active part.

*   *   *

If we now turn to the representation of Mendelist genetics presented by Lysenko in his Report, it will be clear that it is a serious distortion of all the essential points.

First of all it should be noted that no precise reference is ever made to Mendel himself or his works, except with a kind of insinuation attributable to an utterly dishonest epistemological anti-clericalism, stating that he was a monk or ridiculing his experiments on the pretext that he worked on peas. Morgan receives no better treatment: he is constantly called an 'American scientist' and lampooned for wasting his time watching flies. . . .

But, more serious, 'Mendelism-Morganism' is reduced at Lysenko's hands to two extremely general propositions and what he called a 'scholasticism' which is simply abstract and formal deduction from these two propositions.

According to Lysenko, 'classical' genetic theory claims that 'chromosomes contain a special "hereditary substance" which resides in the body of the organism as though in a case and is transmitted to succeeding generations irrespective of the qualitative features of the body and its conditions of life' (op. cit. p. 19). Hence it follows that 'the Mendelist-Morganist theory does not include in the scientific concept "living body" the conditions of the body's life. To the Morganists, environment is only the background – indispensable, they admit – for the manifestation and operation of the various characteristics of the living body, in accordance with its heredity. They therefore hold that qualitative variations in the heredity (nature) of living bodies are entirely independent of the environment, of the conditions of life' (p. 19).

It is just about possible to argue that these formulations might be made to fit some of the earliest definitions of the gene, such as that of Johannsen, or certain idealist philosophical extrapolations which then found support in this new concept, such as those of Karl Pearson.[10] But they conflict with the living practice of geneticists who, like Muller, sought with success to change genes by external agents (X-rays, but also heat and chemical products such as colchicine) and who had even established that Drosophila could transmit hereditarily a special sensitivity to carbon dioxide. To undertake such experiments obviously implied a quite different conception of the 'hereditary substance' and the gene from the one attributed to them by Lysenko.

So where did this 'error' come from?

Reading the Lysenkoists' texts closely, there is no apparent difficulty in answering: it derived from their systematic assimilation

---

[10] Karl Pearson, the author of *The Grammar of Science*, one of Lenin's targets in *Materialism and Empirio-criticism*, who was a statistician, had worked out a purely formal (statistical) theory of heredity based on Mendel's laws. See his articles in *Biometrika*, the journal published in Cambridge that he founded in 1902.

of the Morganist-Mendelist theses to those of August Weismann. Lysenko went so far as to speak of 'Weismannism-Mendelism' and at the end of the history of biology as he summarized it in his Report, he could quote Weismann at length and conclude: 'Hence, according to Weismann, there can be no new formations of the hereditary substance; it does *not* develop with the development of the individual, and is *not* subject to any dependent changes. An immortal hereditary substance, independent of the qualitative features attending the development of the living body, directing the mortal body, but not produced by the latter – that is Weismann's frankly idealistic, essentially mystical conception, which he disguised as "Neo-Darwinism". Weismann's conception has been fully accepted and, we might say, carried further by Mendelism-Morganism' (p. 17).

A passage like this, which has its parallels in all the Lysenkoists' statements, contains in reality two mutually supporting errors: besides the fact that the terms in which Weismann's theory is presented make its actual role in the history of biology inexplicable, the simple identification of Mendel's theses with those of Weismann fails to recognize the radically novel character of the Mendelist works.

Weismann's theory, which had a wide resonance in its day, and one going far beyond the bounds of biology,[11] was a very complex and frequently changing set of experimental works and often adventurous speculations on the nature of life and the destiny of man.

[11] Notably in Freud's work, as Jacques Lacan quite rightly emphasises in his seminar on *Les Écrits techniques de Freud (Le Séminaire livre I*, Editions du Seuil, Paris 1975): 'Freud props up his theory of the libido with what the biology of his day suggests to him. The theory of the instincts cannot fail to take into account a fundamental bipartition between the purposes of the preservation of the individual and those of the continuity of the species. What is in the background is none other than Weismann's theory, some memory of which you should have retained from your time in philosophy classes. This theory, which has not been definitively proved, posits the existence of an immortal substance of the sexual cells. They constitute a unique sexual line by continuous reproduction. The germ plasm is what perpetuates the species and persists from one individual to another. On the contrary, the somatic plasm is a sort of individual parasite which, from the point of view of the reproduction of the species, has sprouted laterally solely to be the bearer of the eternal germ plasm' (p. 139). One can refer for example to Freud's article 'On Narcissism: an Introduction' (*Standard Edition of the Complete Psychological Works of Sigmund Freud*, Hogarth, London 1953–74, Vol. XIV).
Butler's summary of Weismann is well-known: 'The egg has found in the chicken the way to remake an egg.'

Adapting a notion of Naegeli's, Weismann, whom Mendel – need it be said? – could never have known,[12] argued that every organism is made up of two sorts of cells: the germ cells (or 'germen', or 'germ plasm') and the somatic cells (or 'soma'). According to this theory, the germ cells contain a substance composed of a series of hierarchized particles – the 'ides' – of which the chromosomes are the biggest. Each 'ide' in turn conceals smaller parts each of which holds some organ within its dependence: Weismann therefore called them 'determinants'. The individual's germ plasm, inherited from its ancestors, already complete in the fertilized egg which gave it birth, produces during the development of every living being the somatic cells which constitute the whole of the organism as the result of a very complicated mechanism of diffusion of the 'determinants', the fictional details of which Weismann more than once indulged in describing.

But the important thing is the fact that the cells which give birth to the future sexual cells of the adult are exceptional and retain the whole germ plasm in themselves. These sexual cells can thus transmit the plasm intact to the sexual cells which are to begin the cycle again in the next generation.

What emerges from this theoretical structure, erected almost exclusively by deductive methods, is the fact that there is a continuity, even an 'eternity' of the germ plasm, and living organisms can be regarded as each in its turn no more than a 'vehicle' for this plasm: a mere temporary, ephemeral excrescence on the seminal lineage.

Hence finally the idea of heredity that summed up 'Weismannism' for his contemporaries: an organism can only inherit characters innate in its parents. Transmission passing from germ cell to germ cell, the somatic tissues being absolutely separate from the germ cells from the beginning of each development, nothing that affects the 'soma' can rebound on the 'germen': so the characters acquired by the organism during its existence cannot be transmitted to the next generation.

Thus what was remembered above all about Weismann was his declared anti-Lamarckism, and his work was 'naturally' inscribed in the battle still raging at the end of the last century about the

---

[12] Weismann's works post-date 1865. See especially the collection of articles translated as *Essays on Heredity and Kindred Biological Problems*, 2nd edition, two volumes, 1891–2.

question of acquired characters. But, paradoxically, it is in a quite different connection that it has in fact retained a positive place in the actual history of the sciences, via a less immediately apparent aspect of the doctrine, but one which a knowledge of Mendel's work allows us today, recursively, to accord its true value. In fact, by paths of his own, and ones which proved much less fruitful, Weismann, too, *had abandoned, as Mendel had done without anyone yet having realized it, the theoretical schema of 'fusion-heredity'*. He thus removed the main obstacle to the constitution of a scientific theory of heredity, the object which, as we have seen, had blocked Darwin himself. That is why these writings, obscure and involved as they are, and manifestly delirious too in some places, were able to help make possible the 'rediscovery' of Mendel's theses.[13]

But here is the other side of the coin: Weismann, and many others subsequently, following his example, felt justified in drawing from his distinction between 'germen' and 'soma' frankly mystical considerations about the eternity of human nature which were readopted in the racist propaganda of the Nazis. Rosenberg, for example, did not hesitate to make the 'racial soul' which, according to him, had been transmitted unaltered from ancient Germany to our day, the equivalent of the 'germ plasm' transmitted unchanged down the generations.[14]

It is this last aspect of Weismann that Lysenko emphasized: the accusation that it is a 'racist' theory often recurs in his denunciations of Weismannism. It is to this last aspect that he assimilated Mendel's theory when he spoke of 'Weismannism-Mendelism'. By this means he could denounce 'the mystical basis and the racial implications' of classical genetics. But the price was a double

[13] Examples of works which, without producing a single scientific concept, have thus allowed, *through their critical effects*, by 'dislodging' an essential element of a dominant scientific ideology, the formation of a concept to which that ideology was an obstacle, are not uncommon in the history of the sciences. It is obviously a more uncommon case for a work to contribute by such a mechanism to the rediscovery of already constituted scientific concepts which it then proves to have 'lagged behind' . . . but such is the 'Weismann case'.

[14] The English Marxist biologist J. B. S. Haldane had stood out against the racist uses of the results of genetic research in 1937. In his remarkable book *Heredity and Politics*, he revealed the hyperbolae such an exploitation depends on. Marcel Prenant, too, had published an article on the same theme in *La Pensée*, July–August 1939. He wrote, notably, 'True genetics is not racist. It does not set up a mythical image of the gene related to the racial soul. It knows perfectly well and never forgets that between the genotype and the real phenotype there is all the difference that results from the influence of the environment. It also knows all the difficulties in its own application to the human domain.'

mystification, since Weismann's work cannot be reduced to the ideological exploitations it has been subjected to, and there is no natural identity between it and Mendel's theory.

I said: Lysenko gave a distorted picture of Mendelism. It is now possible to specify: by subjecting Mendel's work to a veritable theoretical regression which took it back into its ideological pre-history.

★   ★   ★

Paradoxically, Darwin was no better treated.

To counter what they thought – or pretended to think – is Mendelist genetics, the Lysenkoists presented themselves as defenders of 'Darwinism'. They constantly repeated that Mendelist genetics is a deviation from Darwinism, that it betrays its spirit. Hence it is not enough to have established that their conception of genetics was no better than a crude caricature. The question remains open as to whether they set against this caricature arguments which can, as they claimed, be called 'Darwinist' in some respect or other. If so, the misunderstanding would have been simple and localized: it would only have been a misunderstanding about Mendelism. Lysenko, relying on Darwin, would have been bringing his criticism to bear on a distorted image of Mendel while using arguments which are in fact perfectly compatible with Mendelist theory, which we know is indeed itself not just compatible with but complementary to the Darwinist theory of natural selection. One might then think that Lysenko, for ideological and political reasons, *had repeated in another language* what Mendel had said, turning concepts which are authentically his though disguised in an adopted terminology against a deliberately or unconsciously falsified version of Mendelist science.

This is the interpretation of the Lysenkoist theory that seems, incidentally, to have been adopted by certain Soviet geneticists, probably for tactical reasons: they thought that to defend themselves they needed only to agree wholeheartedly with Lysenko and criticize the 'Weismannist' image of genetics, to dissociate their own work from that image and show that there was no opposition between it and the Lysenkoist theses. It is also the procedure used in 1948 by the geneticist Zhukovskii: 'You say that you have succeeded in converting hard wheat into soft . . . this is training, it is possible, but I will call it mutation, and let Professor Polyakov call me a mutationist' (*Verbatim Report*, p. 461). And later, during a brief exchange with Lysenko, who offered to bring to the platform scores of plants whose parents were vegetative hybrids to prove the truth of his statements, Zhukovskii answered: 'I believe you about those plants. . . . Trofim Denisovich, you never use the term "mutation", you refuse to recognize it. But we do recognize it. And nature supplies the organic world with mutations almost without limit. What causes mutations? On this point, I am entirely with you, Academician Lysenko: environment, external conditions, cause mutations. You call it training' (pp. 463–4).

A merely verbal quarrel? The hypothesis will not withstand the beginnings of a close analysis. And at the same time such an analysis will show why Academician Zhukovskii's 'tactic' was a tragic illusion.

Remember the terms in which Lysenko presented *The Origin of Species*: 'The leading idea of Darwin's theory is the teaching on natural and artificial selection. Selection of variations favourable to the organism has produced, and continues to produce, the fitness which we observe in living nature; in the structure of organisms and their adaptation to their conditions of life. Darwin's theory of selection provided a rational explanation of the fitness observable in living nature. His idea of selection is scientific and true' (ibid., p. 11). Remember, too, that there immediately followed a series of reservations about Darwin's 'errors . . . already pointed out by Engels': 'Darwin's theory, though unquestionably materialist in its main features, is not free of some serious errors' (p. 12). The first of these: 'Along with the materialist principle, Darwin introduced into his theory of evolution reactionary Malthusian ideas' (p. 12).[15]

Lysenko thus proceeded to a division within Darwin's theory: on the one hand, its materialist content, i.e., 'his idea of selection', 'his theory of evolution, which explained the natural causes of the

---

[15] Among other texts, Lysenko quoted Engels's letter to Lavrov of November 12th to 17th 1875: 'The whole Darwinist teaching of the struggle for existence is simply a transference from society to living nature of Hobbes's doctrine of *bellum omnium contra omnes* and of the bourgeois-economic doctrine of competition together with Malthus's theory of population. When this conjurer's trick has been performed (and I question its absolute permissibility, as I have indicated in point 1, particularly as far as the Malthusian theory is concerned), the same theories are transferred back again from organic nature into history and it is now claimed that their validity as eternal laws of human society has been proved.' On the same point, see also *Anti-Dühring*, op. cit., pp. 97–9 and *Dialectics of Nature*, op. cit., pp. 208–9, 235–6.

purposiveness we see in the structure of the organic world' (p. 12);
on the other, his theory of the struggle for existence and his
conception of variation, elements of foreign extraction. The
materialist element is 'a summation of the age-old practical experience of plant and animal breeders' (pp. 11–12), the idealist element: a trace of the dominant bourgeois ideology in the form of a
principle of Malthusian origin.

According to the Lysenkoists, who could appeal on this point to
the violent polemics sparked off by the publication of Darwin's
book, the materialist element of the theory had become the target
for a vigorous bourgeois ideological counter-offensive. Result: this
element had rapidly been lost sight of by biologists themselves, and
in consequence 'Weismannist-Mendelists' had developed unilaterally the idealist element, to the point of giving it the consistency of
a 'theory'.

Thus Lysenko declared: we are the true Darwinists, the heirs to
what is materialist and revolutionary in Darwin's work. We want
to develop and rectify Darwin. The Mendelists' presentation of
themselves as adepts of a 'Neo-Darwinism' which in their case is
no more than a pseudo-scientific system of biological Malthusianism is abusive.

Lysenko's argument might seem strong and his procedure a
formally legitimate one for a Marxist. Darwin's borrowing from
Malthus was not just a daring hypothesis of Engels's, it could be
backed up by Darwin's own testimony: in his *Autobiography*
Darwin stated that he had indeed taken the concept of the struggle
for existence from the author of *An Essay on the Principle of Population*. As for the conclusion Lysenko drew from this – that a 'division'
has to be made between two heterogeneous elements within
Darwin's theory – it might seem in conformity with Lenin's
position on the sciences of nature: is not the 'spontaneous' philosophy of scientists a compromise formation of this kind between
contradictory elements?[16]

However, the Leninist descent of the Lysenkoist intervention in
biology is no more than formal and apparent.

Lysenko relied on Engels; Engels reproduced the letter of
Darwin's *Autobiography*. But it is, to say the least, imprudent, if

[16] Cf. the explanation of this proposed by Althusser in *Philosophie et Philosophie spontanée
des savants (1967)*, François Maspero, Paris 1974, and the illustration vis-à-vis Jacques
Monod that appears in an appendix to it.

one is attempting to think the process of a scientific discovery, to trust blindly the account given of it by the scientist who was its agent, above all when, as here, it is a matter of a retrospective text. In fact, recent studies have shown that, in Darwin's work, the concept of a struggle for existence *pre-existed* his reading of Malthus.[17] But above all, however decisive a part one supposes that Malthus's theory did play in the formation of Darwin's concept of the struggle for existence, it cannot be inferred, as Lysenko inferred, that this concept is *ipso facto* a mere 'transposition' of the Malthusian principle. For that would be to confuse the *process* of a discovery and the theory which is its *result*. The only conclusion that could legitimately be drawn from Darwin's remarks about Malthus is that the Malthusian doctrine served him as a theoretical instrument. But this by no means implies the presence as such of the instrument in the product. The history of the sciences offers many examples to prove that there need be no natural continuity, no theoretical homogeneity between the scientific concept produced and the theoretical instrument which allowed it to be manufactured. A concept does not necessarily carry inscribed indelibly in it the traces of its origin, nor does it reproduce in the domain in which it has been imported its primitive meaning.

This is easily confirmed by a direct comparison between Malthus's principle and Darwin's concept. What in fact is the object of Malthus's demonstration? Malthus aimed to prove, in contradistinction to the Ideologists of the eighteenth century (notably Condorcet) that the intensity and necessity of the struggle prevent any *progress* of the human species. No doubt in Malthus's mind this proposition had a universal value and would, transposed from the human species to others, have led to the affirmation that there is a natural quantitative elimination, *without any selection*. Moreover, whenever Malthus appealed to the notion of the struggle for existence it was not to claim that the superior triumphs: in his eyes the struggle for existence leads to no improvement in a population.[18] So Lysenko was mistaken, as was Engels: Darwin's

[17] I am alluding to the research of Camille Limoges, notably to his important book *La Sélection naturelle*, Presses Universitaires de France, Paris 1970.

[18] On this point, see Yvette Conry's article: 'Darwin et Mendel dans la biologie contemporaine,' *Revue de l'enseignment philosophique*, October–November 1972, and also Camille Limoges's summary: 'Darwinisme et adaptation,' *Revue des questions scientifiques*, July 1970.

principle of the survival of the fittest is clearly *anti-Malthusian*, even if its conception did require the theoretical detour via Malthus.[19]

This mistake of Lysenko's included another: it caused him to miss the *unity* of the theory of evolution, i.e., the fact that the concepts of *adaptation* and *struggle for existence* are interdependent in it. He thus emptied the Darwinian concept of adaptation of its revolutionary content. A theoretically disastrous mistake, since it was precisely in this concept that Darwinism had made its 'break' with the natural history of previous centuries.

In fact, in the Linnaean tradition and even in Lamarck, the notion of adaptation was closely linked to the conception of a 'natural economy'. It was therefore an integral part of a *finalist* conception of the natural order. Thus, when Lamarck used the notion of adaptation he did so to designate the organism's appropriate response to changes in the environment; but a successful response is predetermined by the 'plan of nature', which, in its 'wisdom', foresees the development of the linear 'chain' of beings organized according to a progressive increase in complexity.

Darwin's notion of adaptation, too, is interdependent with a notion of an equilibrium in nature; but (and this is the decisive point) as this equilibrium is achieved *in* and *by* the struggle for the appropriation of the environment, it excludes all predetermination. In other words, the Darwinist concept was revolutionary in that it is non-teleological. It has even proved possible to show that, historically, it was constructed through a long effort to *reject* the classical notion of a 'natural economy'.[20] As is clear, what constitutes the non-finalism of Darwin's theory is its *coupling* of the notion of adaptation to that of struggle: its thinking adaptation as a process in struggle.[21]

But Lysenko said: the struggle for existence is Malthusianism in biology, it is the idealist element in Darwin's theory. Only the

[19] François Jacob himself as well as other historians has fallen victim to the same mistake (cf. *The Logic of Living Systems*, op. cit., pp. 169–70).

[20] In the article referred to above, Limoges shows how Darwin was able to make this rejection by working on the contradictions which 'overdetermined' the notion in William Paley's natural theology.

[21] Georges Canguilhem wrote: 'For Darwin, to live is to submit to the judgement of the totality of living beings an individual difference. This judgement can have two outcomes: either one dies or in one's turn one becomes, for a time, a member of the jury. But so long as one lives one is always jury and judged' (*La Connaissance de la vie*, Vrin, Paris, 2nd edition 1965, p. 137).

notion of adaptation should be retained. As a result he defined adaptation, *in abstraction from struggle*, as an 'adjustment' of the organism to conditions in the external environment in conformity with its needs and nature. But to dissociate adaptation and struggle for existence in this way is to miss what was new in the Darwinist concept of adaptation, to 'forget' what constitutes its scientific character proper; thus it is to make the theory of evolution regress into its ideological pre-history, to a finalist conception of the relationship between the living being and its environment.

*   *   *

Lysenko's infidelity to Darwin does not stop there. He wrote: 'The scientific ideas of Darwinism are a summation of the age-old practical experience of plant and animal breeders' (pp. 11–12), and his supporters constantly made this thesis an argument against their opponents who they attacked for the academic character of their researches, remote from practice. Now, so formulated, this thesis contains a dual historical and theoretical ambiguity which can also find some support in references to the letter of Darwin's texts.

It is indeed true that on several occasions Darwin acknowledged his debt to 'breeders'; we also know that he accumulated a lot of documentation about the artificial selection of animals and plants. But it has also been established that all this documentation only affected the elaboration of the concept of 'natural selection' after the event, as confirmation of an already formed theory. To say that this theory was a 'summation' of the experience of breeders is to commit oneself to an *empiricist* conception of the formation of scientific concepts which does not explain Darwin's actual efforts.

The ambiguity is all the more serious in that it led to an implicit assimilation of the mechanism of natural 'selection' to that of artificial selection. Since the breeder's work is simply to make as judicious as possible a choice amongst the organisms subject to selection as a function of the use to which he intends them, if natural selection is assimilated to artificial selection, if the concept of 'natural selection' becomes a mere generalization of empirical observations made during the work, however 'age-old', of breeders, the idea of such a choice is inevitably introduced *into nature*. Now Darwin, when he defined 'natural selection' – 'This preservation of favourable variations and the rejection of injurious variations I call Natural Selection' – was very careful to explain that this mechanism implies *no choice*, that unlike artificial selection this is a matter of a non-purposive process. It is clear that Darwin only used the term 'selection' because he lacked a better term and, essentially, as a convenient pedagogic analogy.[22] To give this analogy, understood in the strict sense, a theoretical function was, against Darwin's own explicit warnings, to reintroduce purposiveness into a process which does not contain it. This is the path that Lysenko took. It converges with his finalist interpretation of the notion of adaptation and strengthens it. Lysenkoism, whatever it claimed, is thus not a Darwinism. It is even an *anti-Darwinism* insofar as on the central issue – the rejection of finalism – it betrays Darwin.

Indeed, theoretical regression and return to finalism crystallize in the decisive point at which Lysenko came, very 'logically' to contradict Darwin openly: the question of competition within a single species.

As we know, Lysenko denied the existence of such a competition with the utmost energy, seeing in it nothing but a 'fiction' invented by the bourgeoisie to justify the class division of society. Let us recall his specifically 'biological' arguments: 'The rabbit is eaten by the wolf but does not eat other rabbits; it eats grass. Likewise wheat does not crowd wheat out of existence' (*Agrobiology*, op. cit., pp. 512–3). The wolf not being a wolf for the wolf, man could not by nature be a wolf for man. . . .

From this 'theory' Lysenko deduced one of his most famous techniques, the planting in 'clusters' or 'hills' of *kok-sagyz* (Russian rubber dandelion) or forest trees, which the 'Great Plan for the Transformation of Nature' drawn up by Stalin in 1949 was to impose on a vast scale, to the great detriment of Soviet agriculture.

It is worth stopping to look at the texts devoted to this technique – not to sneer complacently at the speculative delirium in which they were eventually trapped but because there Lysenko's finalism reveals all its effects, in such an acute form that it is almost religious. In this sense these texts tell the 'truth' about the whole Lysenkoist theoretical construction.

---

[22] It obviously remains open why Darwin allowed this ambiguity to survive at the terminological level. It certainly seems that it is not a purely verbal question but one which reveals an index of the fact that the work of the break with finalism was not complete in *The Origin of Species*. The theory of pangenesis and its ideological extensions are there for confirmation.

'In order that the weak kok-sagyz plants may be able not only to hold their own in this severe inter-specific struggle but to produce greater crops we have come to their assistance. The collective-farm members have begun to sow kok-sagyz in hills: 100–200 kok-sagyz seeds are placed in one hole and around it $\frac{1}{4}$ sq. m. of free space is left. The weed attacks the hill but on encountering a mighty wall of resistance on the part of the numerous kok-sagyz plants it cannot make its way into the hill. And the kok-sagyz, having rid itself of its worst enemy, keeps on growing in bunches (association) by using up the nutriment and moisture of the entire free space given to it' (ibid., p. 513).

Reporting in 1957 on a conversation he had had with Lysenko on this point in 1949, Marcel Prenant wrote: 'I allowed myself to put a question to him: "I admit that young trees should be planted in a cluster; they may thus be better protected at first; but is it not necessary to remove some of them after a few years?" "No," replied Lysenko, explaining: "They will sacrifice themselves for one." "Do you mean," I replied, "that one will turn out to be stronger and the others will weaken or perish?" "No," he repeated, "they will sacrifice themselves for the good of the species"' (*La Pensée* no. 72, 1957, pp. 23–6; cit. Medvedev, op. cit., p. 168).

For struggle, Lysenko substituted *sacrifice*: theology is decidedly the inseparable companion of teleology. The apparently Marxist justifications cannot mask the religious character of these passages.

Professor Gustav Wetter, obviously very sensitive to this aspect of the doctrine, correctly links it to another central notion of mature Lysenkoism, that of the 'marriage for love' invoked to explain fertilization.[23] Here is a passage from Safonov about wheat: 'The wind carried a cloud of pollen. And from this cloud the plant elects the pollen suitable for it. It does not pollinate itself with just any kind of pollen. It *chooses* its pollen. Only organisms that suit and strengthen each other combine if nature is given a free hand. In this field, among the clipped ears marked with red thread, we, as it were, stood on the threshold across which we could clearly and distinctly see the operation of the most profound, important and beautiful laws that govern all living things on Earth – both

---

[23] Gustav Wetter's book *Dialectical Materialism. A Historical and Systematic Survey of Philosophy in the Soviet Union* (translated by Peter Heath, Routledge and Kegan Paul, London 1958), which is presented as a well-documented history of Soviet philosophy, is a version of lectures given at the Pontificio Instituto Orientale.

animals and plants. We were not surprised at the bold and beautiful words with which Lysenko described what was going on among his wheats: "Marriage for love!"' (op. cit., pp. 237–9).

★   ★   ★

In conclusion, may I emphasize the astonishing consistency of Lysenko's 'errors' in the theory of heredity?

Contrary to what has been claimed, this consistency is by no means due to the inspiration of a clearly understood doctrine such as Lamarckism, the latter supposedly providing the Lysenkoists with a positive reference point in their critique of other theories and in their own investigations. Lamarckism, about which they were strangely discreet, was no better handled by the Lysenkoists than Mendelism or Darwinism: they were completely alien to it.[24]

---

[24] There have been many attempts to see a supposed 'Lamarckism' of Lysenko as the grounds for his deliberate or accidental theoretical 'derailment'. Did he not make the 'inheritance of acquired characters' the emblem of his doctrine?

If we leave the verbal surface for only a moment, it becomes clear that in fact Lysenko was no more a Lamarckist then he was a Darwinist.

In the classical Lamarckist sense, in fact, it was reckoned that there is the inheritance of an acquired character when this character, acquired by one generation under the influence of the environment, is transmitted to the next generation *whatever the environment* in which the latter grows up. Hence to claim that there really has been the transmission of an 'acquired' character, it is necessary at each generation to choose for evidence certain individuals and make them live *in conditions other than* those in which the new character has been acquired; one can then verify whether the character is manifested, and hence whether it has been *acquired* by the organism.

Now the Lysenkoists gave a very different definition of what an acquired character is: 'When an organism finds in its environment the conditions suitable to its heredity,' wrote Lysenko, 'its development proceeds in the same way as it proceeded in previous generations. When, however, organisms do not find the conditions they require and are forced to assimilate environmental conditions which, to some degree or other, do not accord with their nature, then the organisms or sections of their bodies become more or less different from the preceding generation' (*Report*, p. 35). This passage yields the conclusion that, if they are left in *the same environmental conditions* that enabled them to 'acquire' a new character, this character will be transmitted to their descendants.

An example: the explanation given by the Lysenkoist Shaumyan for the creation of a new high-yield breed of cows, the famous Kostroma cows of the 'Karavaevo' sovkhoz: 'For a period of over twenty years the Karavaevo herd received abundant and diversified feed, particularly during the last 10–13 years. Thus, in 1928, the total fodder expenditure per forage-fed cow amounted to 3,256 Russian food units, and in the best years was in excess of 6,000 food units. The expenditure of concentrated fodder per cow was 1,000–2,500 kg. Milkings per forage-fed cow were, correspondingly, 3,389 kg, reaching a maximum in 1940 of 6,310 kg. The live body weight of cows averaged 649 kg for the entire herd' (*Verbatim Report*, p. 254). I will cut short the description of these fabulous cows to jump to Shaumyan's conclusion: 'In the light of these facts, one question is raised: can one accept the Morganists' claim as to the immutability of the sexual cells and the impossibility

The consistency of the Lysenkoists' 'errors' is to be found in the overall *system* of their misconceptions of the doctrines, in the overall system of the falsifications they imposed on the theories which served them both as positive points of reference (Darwin) and as foils (Mendel, Weismann). It is not just their positions vis-à-vis each of these theories taken singly which is pertinent, but rather, throughout these conjugated positions, the *relationship* posited between these theories that becomes significant. To understand the true inspiration of the Lysenkoist theory where heredity is concerned, the logic of this diabolical interplay of reference, exclusion and amalgamation must be recognized.

It all fits together, indeed. Lysenkoism claimed to be Darwinist in order to condemn Mendelist genetics. Certainly. But this opposition was completely misplaced from the start, for not only did Lysenkoism attack a misrepresentation of Mendelist genetics, it did so in the name of a profoundly adulterated version of Darwinist theory. All the elements were falsified from the start, and it is understandable that they made any communication impossible between Lysenko and the geneticists in 1948. Yet it was on this basis that Lysenko 'argued', i.e., in fact developed the logic of his aberrant presuppositions: he had to identify an essential part of Darwin's work arbitrarily with that of Malthus to achieve an amalgamation of Mendel and Weismann. He thus identified Darwin's 'struggle' for existence with Malthus's 'principle of population'. He claimed that Weismann merely developed this supposedly 'idealist' side of Darwin. This eventually allowed him to amalgamate Mendel and Weismann. Darwin, Lysenko's stated positive theoretical point of reference, thus only serves him in his falsified

---

of the inheritance of acquired characters? . . . How can one explain the significance of genes which enable cows, millenia in advance, to give up to 15,000 kgs of milk a year? . . . The development of the cows' udders is indisputable proof of the inheritance of characters acquired under the influence of the surrounding environment. The protracted selection of conditions of existence has made quantitative modifications which, hereditarily transmitted, transform the qualities of the original species' (ibid., pp. 258–60 cit. according to the abridged French version published in *Europe* nos. 33–4, September–October 1948, pp. 86–8).

A more flagrant confusion is unimaginable: all this has nothing to do with the inheritance of acquired characters in the Lamarckist sense; in order to establish the latter, it would precisely have been necessary to have raised some of the second generation of these illustrious cows in quite different conditions to see if the yield persisted. Besides, contrary to what Shaumyan stated, a 'Mendelist' geneticist would have no trouble explaining this case. He could say: however good the genotype may be in some of its possible phenotypes, the phenotype realized will only be really good if it is given sufficient appropriate care.

representation as an appropriate 'theoretical' operator by which to achieve the amalgamation which enabled him to condemn Mendel in the guise of Weismann. . . .

And, since Darwin is the centre of what must really be called this 'operation' literally mounted against Mendel and genetics, since Darwin is the Lysenkoists' sole positive point of reference, it is his *treatment* that reveals to us not only the logic of the operation, but also the Lysenkoists' ultimate inspiration. As we have seen, it is no accident that Lysenko marked himself off from Darwin in the matter of the theory of the 'struggle for existence': once this notion has been removed, the road is wide open to a finalist conception of living nature, and, as the history of modern biology has been made against this conception, the road is wide open for the *restoration* of finalism, which, scientifically, cannot but be a regression.

It is Lysenko himself who bears witness to this interpretation in the extravagant theory of heredity he constantly proposed: 'Heredity is the *property* of a living body to *require* definite conditions for its life and development and to respond in a definite way to various conditions' (ibid., p. 35). This definition, which Marcel Prenant rightly noted in 1948 is literally incomprehensible (heredity as a 'property'? and also as a 'requirement'?), can only be deciphered as the repercussion of a finalist conception of living nature.

Naturally, this finalism, conscious or unconscious, is philosophically charged. And here a new drama comes into play. For after the meeting between Lysenko and Prezent (1935), Lysenko's 'theory' was no longer presented as the interpretation of certain technical results, nor even as one doctrine of finalist inspiration among others; it was presented as the direct *application*, in the domain of biology, of a determinate philosophy, the official philosophy of the Bolshevik Party and the Soviet state, dialectical materialism. No serious examination of the Lysenkoist theory of heredity and its fortunes can elude this fact: between 1935 and 1940 recourse to an established conception of dialectical materialism, to its ideological and political powers, played a theoretically and historically decisive part in the constitution and justification of the doctrine. And it was this 'pedigree' that was recognized and made official by the decisions of 1948.

We must therefore now confront this question, which is the one that arouses the most lively controversy.

5

The Theory of the 'Two Sciences' and State Ideology

In his preface to the French edition of Medvedev's book, Monod writes:

'What for me was the most revealing aspect of these astonishing documents was the fact that the real debate did not concern experimental biology itself, but almost exclusively ideology or rather dogmatics. The essential argument (ultimately the only one) tirelessly repeated by Lysenko and his supporters against classical genetics was *its incompatibility with dialectical materialism*. This was the real debate, the heart of the problem, and on this terrain chosen by Lysenko but which they could not avoid, the Russian geneticists were clearly beaten from the start. For it is perfectly true that the ultimate basis of classical genetics, the theory of the gene, invariant from generation to generation and even through hybridizations, is incompatible with the spirit and the letter of the dialectics of nature according to Engels. So, moreover, is the purely selective theory of evolution, already formally denied by Engels himself. It was easy, on the contrary, to show – and Lysenko tirelessly returned to this too – that Michurinist biology, by "proving" the inheritance of acquired characters and the influence of the environment on material heredity, precisely paralleled materialist dialectics, glorified it with new and fabulous discoveries, and made way for a real biological "parousia".'

This passage is echoed in *Chance and Necessity* when Monod denounces in Marxism an up-to-date form of 'animism'. To support this condemnation factually and illustrate the 'epistemological disaster' to which he thinks Marxist philosophy would inevitably expose the natural sciences, he resorts once again to the 'Lysenko affair':

'Lysenko accused geneticists of maintaining a theory radically opposed to dialectical materialism, and therefore necessarily false. Despite the disclaimers of Soviet geneticists, Lysenko was perfectly right: the theory of the gene as the hereditary determinant, invariant from generation to generation and even through hybridizations, is indeed completely irreconcilable with dialectical principles.'[1]

During the great debate which followed the appearance of this book, the Marxists did not to my knowledge reply on this point. It was easy to criticize his 'natural philosophy'[2] *for its effects,* denouncing the political implications of his theoretical positions; especially so since Monod had made no mystery of them and had frankly and clearly stated them in the last chapter of his work. In fact, a, whole army of commentators, Marxists in the forefront, have dissected and attacked the few pages Monod devotes to his conception of socialism. But what has one achieved when one has 'brought out' the anti-Marxism of an author . . . who states it plainly? Who does one hope to convince by this kind of exorcism?

It was more difficult to sort out in Monod's philosophical apparatus the theses which derived from his actual scientific practice and those which were no more than the shadow cast by his ideological positions; and to study their original combination within it. A few have ventured this, with the idea that they might make scientists – and especially biologists – realize the 'spontaneous' *materialism* of their scientific practice and thus enable them to resist the idealist exploitation of the results of the new biology by the ruling ideology.[3]

However, there remain his *factual arguments.* And foremost among them: Lysenko. Willynilly, these arguments give Monod's positions force and an audience. Not to answer them is to allow real and not imaginary motives for scientists' persistent distrust of Marxist philosophy to survive intact.

Yes, it must be conceded to Monod (and all those who share his position) that he has hit the nail on the head: it was indeed in the name of a conception of dialectical materialism that the Michurinist theory of heredity was erected after 1935; it was indeed this con-

---

[1] *Chance and Necessity,* translated by Austryn Wainhouse, Collins, London 1972, p. 46.

[2] The work's sub-title is 'An Essay on the Natural Philosophy of Modern Biology'.

[3] This is what Louis Althusser, for example, had attempted, basing his argument on the text of Monod's inaugural lecture at the Collège de France. The text of this analysis is to be found in *Philosophie et Philosophie spontanée des savants,* op. cit.

ception of Marxist philosophy which was charged to unify its criticisms of Mendelism, to provide a foundation for its own concepts and to give a theoretical form to this delirious doctrine.

Need I quote more texts?

Lysenko himself never missed an opportunity to stress the organic link between his materialist philosophical positions and his 'scientific' concepts. 'Stalin's teaching about gradual, concealed, unnoticeable quantitative changes leading to rapid, radical qualitative changes permitted Soviet biologists to discover in plants the realization of such qualitative transitions, the transformation of one species into another,' he wrote in 1953 (cit. Medvedev, op. cit., p. 134). And already, in his 1948 Report, he had stated: 'The materialist theory of the evolution of living nature necessarily presupposes the recognition of hereditary transmission of individual characteristics acquired by the organism under definite conditions of its life; it is unthinkable without recognition of the inheritance of acquired characters' (*Report*, p. 15). Glushchenko went further: 'Soviet biologists, mastering *the science of all sciences*, the Marxist dialectical method, and accumulating experimental material, are exposing the idealist essence of the Morgan teaching' (*Verbatim Report*, p. 218). The philosopher Mitin, who built his intervention on a criticism of a book by the geneticist Shmal'gauzen (or Schmalhausen), set out to prove that 'the entire methodology upon which this book rests has nothing in common with dialectical materialism' (ibid., p. 269), and on the contrary 'demonstrated' that 'Michurin's theory is a striking illustration of the application of materialist dialectics in scientific research' (p. 275).

Stoletov ended his pamphlet[4] with the words: 'In their researches, the Michurinists are guided by the only correct conception of the world, the conception of dialectical materialism, the great doctrine of Marx, Engels, Lenin and Stalin. This is where lie both the factor behind the past successes of the Michurinists and the promise of even more important successes for Michurinist biology in the future.'

Is there, finally, any need to recall that outside the Soviet Union it was philosophical arguments that were put forward to defend or impose Lysenkoism? Thus, to take only one example, in 1950 Francis Cohen justified the rejection of the concept of mutation by

4 *Mendel ou Lyssenko?*, op. cit., p. 58.

subjecting it directly to the judgement of a certain conception of dialectics: 'Suddenly,' he wrote, 'a gene changes, and as a result, a character changes too. There has been a sudden leap, a discontinuity, a dialectical phenomenon. But where is the accumulation of quantitative changes leading to the sudden qualitative leap, since the mutation is fortuitous, unpredictable, undirectable?... Perfectly accurate phenomena observed by Mendelist scientists are converted into nonsense because they refuse to place them in the environment of surrounding conditions.'[5]

★   ★   ★

There is no escape from this undeniable *statement of fact*; it could be bolstered by many more quotations. But it is also evident that this statement of fact implies that we Marxist philosophers have a duty to settle accounts with the past we have inherited; and are under an imperious necessity, if we simply want to be heard in the ideological battle, to prove that we are capable of *analyzing* in our own concepts the errors that were committed in this past, risking all that we know or think that we know about Marxist philosophy in so doing.

This being so, we cannot be satisfied with the incredible *silence* that has surrounded Lysenko's name in the Soviet Union in the more than ten years since he left the centre of the stage. For, with the exception of the polemical articles written in the 1960's by the geneticists, at considerable risk to themselves, to hasten the end of the misadventure, with the exception of the catastrophic assessments then published by the agronomists of the results of the experiments made under Lysenko's leadership since the War, *there has been no overall critical examination of the doctrine in the USSR*. In particular, no philosopher, as far as I know, has undertaken to draw the lessons *for dialectical materialism itself* of the interpretation then given of it and the practice it inspired.

This silence is disastrous, for not only does it provide arguments to the opponents of Marxism, it also has profound effects on the contemporary practice of Marxist philosophy, which is still, even in the form of the most sincere denials, haunted and marked by a past which it has been unable or ill-equipped to liquidate theoretically.

[5] In the collection *Science bourgeoise et science prolétarienne*, op. cit.

I shall therefore take a hard look, at the cost of restricting myself for the time being to another statement of fact.

Here it is.

We must admit that, if historical materialism, the science of the history of social formations the 'cornerstones' (Lenin) of which were laid down by Marx in *Capital*, has been tested, developed and corrected by the political practice and theoretical reflection of the workers' movement to the point at which it can present itself today as a body of concepts consistent enough to receive every day the sanction of the gigantic 'experimentation' constituted in its various forms by the class struggle of the proletariat against imperialism, Marxist philosophy, dialectical materialism, is in a quite different situation: one hundred years after the Eleventh Thesis on Feuerbach, it remains in a state of theoretical non-elaboration such that the question of its (theoretical) existence can still be asked. The diagnosis made by Althusser in the introduction to *For Marx* ten years ago now is still correct in essentials: 'Marxist philosophy, founded by Marx in the very act of founding his theory of history, has still largely to be constituted' (NLB, London 1977, pp. 30–31).

Certainly it is not on a blank page that I shall have to inscribe the first words of a doctrine still in intellectual limbo. I know that there are works of Marxist philosophy, some of them written by leaders of the workers' movement, too; far be it from me to belittle Engels's books dealing with philosophy, Lenin's interventions or Mao's essays, to cite only those examples. I know that there are also 'textbooks' of Marxist philosophy (such as Politzer's in France); nor is it a question of denying the function they have had in the theoretical and political formation of the best working-class militants, who have found in them and still do find in them an approach to questions which the bourgeois forms of the division of manual and intellectual labour close to them.

What I mean is that the expression 'dialectical materialism', far from designating a unified theoretical whole, has covered and still covers profoundly *contradictory* philosophical conceptions.

Let me specify.

The materialist and dialectical philosophical theses set to work by Marx in the elaboration of the basic concepts of historical materialism, by Engels in his polemic against Dühring, by Lenin in the heat of ideological and political battle against Bogdanov and the 'Otzovists' and then in the constitution of the theory of imperialism, by Gramsci in his tireless debate with Croce's spiritualism, by Mao in his struggle against dogmatist and empiricist tendencies in the Chinese Communist Party . . . have always had manifestly *critical* effects: they all used them as 'weapons' to 'knock away' the obstacles in theory which were, in a particular conjuncture, blocking the process of scientific and political practice. In each case the role of these theses was to open to theory the space of a 'play' that allowed them to master in thought the nature and the displacement of contradictions to which practice had to adjust in order to transform its object.

But it must be recognized that alongside this interpretation of the theses of dialectical materialism, the Marxist tradition has handed down to us another, which I shall call not just 'dogmatic', in the sense that it fixes thought around immutable and inactive notions, but also *ontological*,[6] in the sense that it 'realizes' the determinations of philosophy itself in 'being'.

This interpretation is not a late avatar or even only a historically dated version of dialectical materialism; in reality it has accompanied it throughout its history and often coexists with the first in the same works.[7] But what is more serious, *for more than forty years it has been imposed as the dominant version of Marxist philosophy*, to the point that it has been identified with it and poses as a veritable 'orthodoxy'.

I say 'orthodoxy' not to pronounce a judgement for the sake of vain polemic but to take cognisance of a *fact*: this interpretation was codified and put on record by Stalin in 1938 in a book which very quickly came to be used as the only real text book of Marxist philosophy in the Soviet Union and the whole world, and served for years as an almost exclusive reference for works of philosophy, which were very often no more than commentaries on it or illustrations of it: this is the chapter of *The History of the Communist Party* (*Bolshevik*) entitled 'Dialectical and Historical Materialism'.

Nothing is more instructive for grasping the essence of what I have called the 'ontological' interpretation of dialectical materialism

[6] This terminology was already used by Etienne Balibar in the lecture he gave last year (1975) at the Centre d'Etudes et de Recherches Marxistes on 'Dialectique des luttes de classes et lutte de classe dans la dialectique' (to be published by the CERM).

[7] This is the case with several of Engels's writings and especially the incomplete developments of *Dialectics of Nature*, the formulae of which constitute the main reservoir of the 'quotations' which the ontological interpretation of dialectical materialism has deployed as arguments for nearly half a century.

than to compare Stalin's statements with the Leninist theses from which he claims authorization. I shall do it on one particular point, though obviously a crucial one: the conception of dialectics.

In his notes *On the Question of Dialectics* (1915), Lenin wrote, summarizing once again the lessons he had drawn from reading Hegel: 'The condition for the knowledge of all processes of the world in their "*self-movement*", in their spontaneous development, in their real life, is the knowledge of them as a unity of opposites. Development is the "struggle" of opposites' (*Collected Works*, Vol. 38, Lawrence and Wishart, London 1961, p. 360). Stalin on the other hand wrote: 'The dialectical method of apprehending nature . . . regards the phenomena of nature as being in constant movement and undergoing constant change, and the development of nature as the result of the interaction of opposed forces in nature' (*Problems of Leninism*, op. cit., p. 570).

Here are two apparently concordant texts: Stalin's fidelity to Lenin's philosophical positions seems indubitable at first glance. Yet a closer examination reveals that the passage from Stalin makes a slide from one conception of dialectical materialism – the critical conception of the practice of its theses – to another: the ontological conception of its supposed 'laws'.

What Lenin stated as 'a condition for knowledge' of the processes of the world has been turned by Stalin into *a law of the world itself*, inscribing in being the (philosophical) presupposition of its knowledge. The fundamental dialectical thesis of the unity of opposites, whose function, according to Lenin, is to enable the process of the scientific knowledge of nature (and society) to overcome the idealist mystifications that tend to fix its results in so many 'absolutes', which thus enables knowledge to advance, has become in Stalin a law of nature itself (and society) which human knowledge only has to 'mirror' to be 'valid'.

In other words, a dialectical philosophical *thesis* which opens to objective knowledge the field of its own investigation according to its own modalities, is turned by the 'Stalinist' ontological interpretation of dialectical materialism into a general 'law' which is supposed to state the *universal form* of the laws established by the sciences of nature. It is called a 'law' ('law of dialectics') because it is held to be theoretically homogeneous with the laws stated by the sciences, and is conceived with them as the model. In return, each of these laws – notably those of historical materialism – is supposed to give a 'concrete' content to this form vis-à-vis its own object; each actual science thus presenting itself as the *application* to a special domain of the general 'law'. In short, the thesis governing the contradictory movement of the appropriation of being by thought on the basis of their respective movements is transformed, in these circumstances, into a law of movement of being which, according to an empiricist conception of knowledge, will be uncovered by reflection in thought.[8]

The first incalculable consequence of this transition to an ontological conception of dialectical materialism was clearly stated in *Dialectical and Historical Materialism*: the dialectics installed in being is transformed into a principle of evolution. As a result, Stalin's text, formulating the 'principal features of the dialectical method' under four heads, really outlined the pattern of an *evolutionist* conception of dialectics.

'The dialectical method . . . holds that the process of development should be understood not as movement in a circle, not as a simple repetition of what has already occurred, but as an onward and upward movement, as a transition from an old qualitative state to a new qualitative state, as a development from the simple to the complex, from the lower to the higher' (op. cit., p. 571).

It is clear how Lysenko, who relied on this interpretation of dialectical materialism, could have found in it a philosophical foundation for his biological 'finalism'; it is understandable that from 1935 on he could have presented his 'theory of the phasic development of plants' as a direct 'application' of dialectical materialism. For indeed his agronomic theory and this version of

[8] The correlate to this empiricist conception of knowledge is a *pragmatist* conception of truth which misses the point of the Leninist thesis of the 'criterion of practice' to find in the immediacy of success a guarantee of the truth and in the immediacy of failure an assurance of the falsity of a theory. In the name of this thesis, as we have seen, the Mendelist science of heredity was required to authenticate its scientific status by applications it was not yet in a position to provide, not through any internal vice but for lack of sufficiently developed conceptual instruments; it was refused the time that every science needs to become effective. Inversely, if a technique has proved more or less effective, the theory claiming to account for it, ill-founded as it may be, is immediately graced with the name of science (Lysenko). Lenin had a quite different conception of the criterion of practice and of the relation between theory and practice: by thinking them as a *process* in which the time of verification plays an essential part, he disengaged them from the arbitrary immediacy which can sanctify any imposture. Moreover, by constantly returning to the idea of the *fruitfulness of failure*, by granting an undoubted *privilege* to *failure* over success, by thus unbalancing the success-failure couple, he went against the stream not only of any pragmatism but also of any positivism of practice.

dialectical materialism were in *harmony*, both being based on the same finalism.

★   ★   ★

But this is not all: his notion of heredity, too, could find justification in this same philosophical conception. Read on in Stalin: 'Contrary to metaphysics, dialectics does not regard nature as an accidental agglomeration of things, of phenomena, unconnected with, isolated from, and independent of, each other, but as a connected and integral whole, in which things, phenomena are organically connected with, dependent on and determined by, each other. The dialectical method therefore holds that no phenomenon in nature can be understood if taken by itself, isolated from *surrounding* phenomena, inasmuch as any phenomenon in any realm of nature may become meaningless to us if it is not considered in connection with surrounding conditions, but divorced from them' (ibid., p. 570).

The expression '*surrounding* conditions', which constantly recurs in Stalin's writings, could not but be taken as the philosophical justification for the Lysenkoist conception of the relation between the environment (the surrounding condition in the biological domain) and the organism. Can it be denied that such a concept of dialectics did indeed underly the Michurinist theory of heredity? Francis Cohen was perfectly right when, quoting these lines of Stalin's, he 'applied' it to Lysenkoism, demonstrating their agreement: 'In this way perfectly accurate phenomena observed by Mendelist scientists are converted into nonsense because they refuse to place them in the environment of *surrounding conditions*. In this way Mendelist heredity is incapable of explaining evolution, because it refuses to make it depend on the environment except via the sieving of already existing forms, whereas the Michurinists, studying and using the fact that the organism and its environment are dependent on, determined by each other, cannot only explain evolution but make species evolve.'

Yes, Lysenkoism is the most illuminating example of an 'application' of dialectical materialism to the sciences of nature: it is precisely the truth of this conception of dialectical materialism that conceives its philosophical theses *as 'laws' to 'apply'* . . . that, against the living practice of materialist and dialectical theses, sets itself up as a judge of actual scientific practice, i.e., inexorably subjects scientific concepts to the jurisdiction of philosophical categories conceived as 'laws'.

*   *   *

So true is this that it is easy to show how this conception of dialectical materialism was able to *unify* theoretically the biological finalism of the Lysenkoist theory of heredity and the technicism of Stalinist politics which, as we have seen, 'called forth' the constitution of such a theory.

This is made even clearer if we return to Stalin's text: once he had presented the essential principles of dialectical materialism (the '*general* theory of the Marxist–Leninist Party'), he demonstrated their '*extension*' and '*application*' to 'social life' and the 'history of societies'.

The picture given of the succession of 'social systems' is, in conformity with the principle recalled above, presented as a development running from lower to higher: 'the slave system would be senseless, stupid and unnatural under modern conditions,' but it represented an 'advance' on the primitive communal system. Similarly, 'when tsarism . . . existed, . . . a bourgeois, democratic republic would have meant a step forward' (ibid., p. 573).

As we see, the law of the evolution (the law of the 'advances') of history is based *in nature* (a regression would be 'unnatural'). But what is this 'nature' which thus orients the movement of history and gives it its purposiveness, what are the material 'conditions' which make its achievement irreversible?

They are to be sought, answered Stalin, not in 'men's ideas', in their 'consciousness' or in their 'theories', nor in the 'environment' constituted by the 'nature which surrounds society', nor finally in the 'growth of population'. For although all these conditions influence 'the development of society', 'facilitate or retard' it, they are not the determining force.

The determining force is 'the method of procuring the means of life necessary for human existence, the mode of production of material values – food, clothing, footwear, houses, fuel, instruments of production, etc. – which are indispensable for the life and development of society' (ibid., p. 583).

It will be said that a more 'classical' position than this one could not be proposed, that it does no more than summarize in a popular manner the principles of historical materialism as they appear in

Capital. Of course. But what is important is the analysis Stalin made of this 'mode of production of material values'; to be precise of the relationship within it between the two 'elements' in play in it: the 'productive forces' and the 'relations of production'. Now, relying on an interpretation that accentuates the already theoretically ambiguous character of the *Preface* to *A Contribution to the Critique of Political Economy* (Marx, 1859), he proposed that it is the productive forces which are 'the most mobile and revolutionary element of production' (ibid., p. 585) and that 'while their development is dependent on the development of the productive forces, the relations of production in their turn react upon the development of the productive forces, accelerating or retarding it' (ibid., p. 586).

Stalin exploited the ambiguity of Marx's text[9] to establish a

[9] The passage from Marx that Stalin quotes at length at the end of his exposition certainly is ambiguous. The mode in which it presents the relationship between *productive forces* and *relations of production* is that of *content* and *form*, which suggests at once that there is a determination of the form by the content: the content acquiring an adequate 'corresponding' form; that there is a relative *stability* and *autonomy* of the form within which the content changes; and that this natural difference (development of the content, stability of the forms which this content has acquired) induces the revolutionary contradiction. This being so one cannot but wonder what is this content that develops *by nature* and this form that remains stable *by nature* unless it is revolutionized by the content. The terms of the question contain those of the answer: it will be the 'spontaneous development' of the productive forces that will be mentioned as the 'motor' of social revolutions and hence of history. In fact, this 'brilliant definition' of historical materialism given by Marx in the *Preface* to *A Contribution to the Critique of Political Economy* has the, to say the least, curious characteristic that it accounts for historical development without saying a word about social classes! and only evokes the class struggle in veiled terms, restricting it to the superstructure and 'becoming conscious'. This insistence on the evolutionist dialectics of content and form, the silence about social classes and the class struggle in the infrastructure produce an almost inevitable reading effect: it is not the class struggle discussed in the *Manifesto* that is the motor of history but, via the content/form dialectics, the 'development of the productive forces'. Here we are on the terrain of the 'economistic-evolutionist' interpretation of Marxism. For in reality the *form-content* couple accounts very poorly for the relationship between the productive forces and the relations of production, simply because it does not account for the fact that the productive forces *too* have the character of social relations and the relations of production are not just forms, external to their content.

To escape the theoretical dead-end of the content/form contradiction, a *different* conception of the unity of the relations of production and the productive forces must be found and the point at which this unity *locks together* must be grasped: in class exploitation. Then not only do the relations of production appear as what they are, class relations putting their *mark* on all the processes of production and the productive forces themselves (the division of labour, labour organization), but also *exploitation* emerges as the basis for all class struggle and the class struggle, no longer a derived phenomenon, becomes the site at which the contradiction productive forces/relations of production locks together and can be unlocked.

This is what *Capital* is able to demonstrate, precisely by abandoning the contradiction between form and content . . .

relationship of *content* to *form* between the productive forces and the relations of production: the development of the content, coming into contradiction with the form in an almost Hegelian manner, 'requires' (a Lysenkoist term) a new form. All he now had to explain was the development of the content itself, its 'motor': this is '*the development and improvement of the instruments of production*', technical progress. The general movement of history is thus explained, from this standpoint, by the progressive improvement of the instruments of production which men use to appropriate 'surrounding nature'.

Evolutionism and technicism thus constitute a theoretical circle, and this circle accounts at once for the birth, the survival and the precise theoretical form taken by the Lysenkoist theory of heredity. The edifice finds a satisfactory keystone in an ontological conception of dialectical materialism, the dominant version of Marxist philosophy which in its categories justifies the 'application' to particular sciences of general 'laws' which are themselves reflected in an evolutionist-finalist theory of nature and history.

*   *   *

Yet if it went no further than this statement of fact – that there is a *harmony*, even a dual one, between Lysenkoism and a determinate conception of dialectical materialism – our analysis would still be insufficient, since it would ignore what everyone saw as the original (and for many, shocking) philosophical character of Lysenko's theory, i.e., the fact that this theory, an 'application' of dialectical materialism, was also immediately presented as a 'science of a new type' and claimed the status of a 'proletarian science', linking the ontological version of the materialist and dialectical theses to the ideological theme of the class character of science in what might be called an '*epistemological voluntarism*' in which application is converted into 'creation'.

Once again, it must be recognized that the Lysenkoists did not have to 'force' the texts or 'twist' the theses they took as their authorization: the interpretation of dialectical materialism that they invoked does imply a *normative* conception of the relationship between Marxist philosophy and the sciences – a conception one of the logical conclusions from which is indeed the absurd theory of the 'two sciences'.

If indeed the 'laws' of dialectics are conceived as the 'laws' of all scientific laws, because dialectics – 'object' of the 'science' with the same name – is inscribed in being as its 'law', all objective knowledges have to be accepted as 'applications' of these 'laws', even if this application has quite obviously been carried out unconsciously in most cases. Hence two complementary philosophical tasks. The first is to put all the sciences through an 'examination' by dialectical materialism to correct, if need be, the scientific 'inconsistencies' which may have arisen from their philosophical 'unconsciousness'. The second: when a constituted scientific discipline proves resistant to translation into the schemata of the supposed 'laws' of dialectics – as was the case with 'Mendelist' genetics – to (re)construct that science on the basis of those 'laws', forging new 'scientific' concepts adequately 'deduced' from Marxist philosophical categories.[10]

It is then enough to 'complement' this theoretical construction, which applies to the sciences and treats philosophy as the 'science of sciences', with the 'classical' thesis that sees in the philosophical opposition between materialism and idealism an expression of a class contradiction and to add that dialectical materialism represents the 'point of view' of the proletariat in philosophy, for the thesis of the *class character of science itself* to impose itself straightaway as the inevitable conclusion to the argument: an intrinsic class character which does not now appear as the 'enrolment of science' (Marx) in the service of capital, but is attached to the essential principles of its methodology and thus has effects in the constitution of its basic concepts and its theory. In these conditions, this thesis, too, has an inevitable corollary: 'proletarian science' has to be counterposed to 'bourgeois science' as the true science, conscious of its progress, to 'pseudo-science', limited in its advances by the class horizons within which it emerged.

In fact, it was one of the constant themes of Lysenkoist propaganda after 1935 to proclaim Lysenkoism as the 'sole authentic science' of hereditary phenomena, arguing at once *both* from its conformity to dialectical materialism *and* from its character as a

---

[10] As is well known, Lenin always and with the utmost rigour opposed such 'deductions'. In *Materialism and Empirio-criticism* he was concerned to show vis-à-vis the question of *matter* that the philosophical category of matter (which appears in the fundamental materialist philosophical *thesis* of the primacy of being over thought) must be distinguished from the scientific concept of matter studied by specialists in the physico-chemical sciences. He showed that confusion between concept and category was the cause of the supposed 'crisis' of modern physics. Later, reading Deborin's statement that 'dialectical materialism provides an answer . . . to the question of the structure of matter', Lenin underlined '*of the structure of matter*' and wrote in the margin 'inexact' (*Collected Works* Vol. 38, op. cit., p. 477).

'proletarian science', which came to the same thing in this completely integrated 'logic'. We can also now understand the tactic used by Lysenko against the 'Mendelists' and later adopted by others in other domains: proceeding by appeals and injunctions he demanded of them 'partisanship in science' and the renunciation of their 'objectivity', echoing but misconceiving two formulae of Lenin's.[11]

It is clear that this argument is generally applicable and that if its premises are accepted, the applicability must be extended to all the sciences of nature. This was seen in June 1947 when, on the occasion of an examination by the Central Committee of Aleksandrov's textbook *A History of Western European Philosophy*, the Party leadership, represented in this case by A. Zhdanov, demonstrated its acceptance of all these philosophical positions.

The most direct and spectacular result of this decision was the 'historic' Session of August 1948 and the adoption of Lysenkoism as the official doctrine where heredity is concerned. But the result was also to install Lysenko's theory as the prototype of a general reconstruction of scientific disciplines on the same philosophical foundations. All the ideological powers of the state apparatus were mobilized to this effect.

Naturally, philosophers and philosophy teachers were in the forefront.

A few days after the Session of the Academy of Agricultural Sciences, the Academy of Sciences' Institute of Philosophy met,

---

[11] Lenin never used the words partisanship *in science* as the Lysenkoists did, but only *partisanship in philosophy*: he called on scientists to be partisan in philosophy in order to disengage the materialist content of their actual practice from the idealist philosophical exploitations to which it is subjected by the dominant ideology. The Lysenkoists, regarding science as a 'historically relative ideology' (J. T. Desanti), interpreted the history of the sciences as a progressive evolution *of* the objectivity of knowledges linked to the class conditions of their production. That is why 'bourgeois science' could never be more than approximately a science. By this means they fell into the *relativism* for which Lenin denounced Bogdanov. These are not inconsequential 'nuances'. When he criticized the 'objectivism' of bourgeois sociology, e.g., in 'What the Friends of the People Are' (*Collected Works*, Vol. 1, Lawrence and Wishart, London 1960), Lenin was very careful to distinguish between the materialist philosophical thesis of *objectivity* which states that scientific knowledges *are* objective and that they develop, correct and complement one another *in the element of objectivity* (a thesis whose function is to prohibit any *relativism*) on the one hand, and on the other the 'objectivist' conception of social phenomena by which the ideologists of the bourgeoisie attribute an unduly objective value to their (class) 'perception' of reality. As I have just recalled, Lysenkoists deny the absolute character of the objectivity thesis under cover of denouncing the objectivism of the scientists.

with several of the most eminent Lysenkoist agronomists present. On the agenda of the meeting: the elaboration of a programme of publications to popularize 'the philosophical basis of the results of the Session' that had just ended. Aleksandrov, the director of the Institute, emphasized 'the enormous scope of this conference' and set out to prove that the 'new Soviet biology' corresponded completely with the spirit of Marxist-Leninist philosophy. This meeting was followed in 1949 by an 'All-Union Conference of Teachers of Marxism-Leninism and Philosophy in Establishments of Higher Education in all the Republics of the Soviet Union'. Its official object: 'On the Situation in the Teaching of Marxism-Leninism and Philosophy and on the Measures Necessary for its Improvement'. But starting with the Report presented by Kaftanov, the Minister of Higher Education, almost the only subject of discussion was biology. Philosophy teachers were critized for having failed to intervene with sufficient energy on Lysenko's side, having failed to grasp what was really at stake in the debate, and having erred in the direction of 'objectivism' and 'cosmopolitanism'. The same terms recurred in the final resolution of the Conference, addressed to Stalin: 'We shall allow ourselves to be guided unfailingly by your directives on the strict maintenance of the unity between theory and practice, philosophy and politics, on the Bolshevist principle of the party spirit in theory. . . . We promise you to demonstrate our Bolshevik and intransigent vigilance towards any manifestation of bourgeois objectivism and cosmopolitanism.'

These declarations did not remain mere words. As is well known, indeed, in subsequent months there developed as applications of these principles, in the name of the same philosophical theses, a Lysenkoist movement which rapidly affected all scientific disciplines.

In biology itself, in 1950 Olga Lepeshinskaya's studies of the origin of cells, begun in 1933, were approved by the Academy of Sciences and her critique of cellular theory as an 'idealist bourgeois theory' was officially endorsed.[12] At the same time a violent dispute

---

[12] Olga Lepeshinskaya had undertaken to study the birth of cells from acellular living matter. Her work, inspired by the few passages on the question in Engels's *Anti-Dühring* and *Dialectics of Nature* – passages copied from Haeckel, incidentally – concerned the development of the chicken embryo. Lepeshinskaya thought she had shown the formation in the yolk of a fertilized egg of protein granules which aggregated into spherulae and

arose about quantum mechanics: Markov, who had propagated the works of the Copenhagen school in the Soviet Union, was treated as a 'philosophical centaur' wishing to reconcile materialism and idealism.[13] Next the theory of relativity was attacked: Einstein was treated as a 'Machist' and as late as 1953 it was still possible to find Maksimov writing that 'the theory of relativity is manifestly anti-scientific'![14] Cybernetics was denounced in the same year in the *Literaturnaya Gazeta* as a 'science of obscurantists'. Pauling's studies on the nature of the chemical bond and molecular structure which gained him the Nobel Prize for Chemistry in 1954 were also taxed with 'Machism' starting in the Autumn of 1949. Chelintsev, who aimed to become the Lysenko of chemistry, therefore undertook to reconstruct the whole of organic chemistry on the basis of dialectical materialism. . . .[15]

In 1950, the Institute of Organic Chemistry of the Academy of Sciences published a Report which stated: 'The crisis of bourgeois science, connected with the general crisis of the capitalistic system, has been illustrated by the theoretical concepts of organic chemistry now being developed by bourgeois scientists and has led to the appearance of methodologically faulty concepts, which are slowing down the further development of science' (cit. Graham, op. cit., p. 305).

This whole campaign was orchestrated by the journal *Voprosy Filosofiii (Problems of Philosophy)* which had recently replaced *Pod*

---

then developed towards the form of nucleated cells. It is obvious why these studies were exhumed and celebrated in this way in 1950: they added one more argument against the Weismannist notion of the continuity and independence of the 'germ plasm'; hence they were grist to the Lysenkoists' mill, in their opinion at least, against Mendelism.

[13] Apart from Maksimov's texts against Markov in the *Literaturnaya Gazeta* which indicted the bourgeois 'anthropomorphism' of quantum mechanics, it seems, as Graham suggests, that the discussions set off by the works of the Copenhagen school were of a high scientific and philosophical calibre, analogous to those that took place in other countries.

[14] A. A. Maksimov, carried away by his zeal and a victim to his own ignorance, went so far as to reject in the name of dialectical materialism any notion of relativity, including Galilean relativity. 'This judgement that a body does not have an objective, given trajectory, existing independently from the choice of system of coordinates,' he wrote, 'is completely anti-scientific . . .'! (*Voprosy Filosofii*, 1948 no. 3, cit. Graham, op. cit., p. 116).

[15] Graham goes into great detail on Chelintsev's 'new chemistry' (ibid., pp. 297–323). It should be added that this is the only case in the sciences of nature in which, as in biology, a new theory with scientific pretensions was constructed at this time. But, as Graham shows, this theory was no more than a reproduction of Pauling's with a different terminology.

Znamenem Marksizma (Under the Banner of Marxism). Its editorial board had been reorganized for this purpose, and its editor, Bonifatii Kedrov, removed for having permitted the publication not only of an article by Markov in support of the Copenhagen school, but also of a text by Shmal'gauzen, one of the most famous of the Mendelists, probably the one most violently attacked at the Session of the Academy of Agricultural Sciences.

Thus a general movement of 'critical re-examination' of the sciences was launched by the official adoption of the 'epistemological voluntarism of application' implied by Stalin's ontological version of dialectical materialism. This is hardly surprising: it was an inevitable consequence.

⋆   ⋆   ⋆

Yet there remains a question which might seem to form an objection to the preceding analyses. For it could rightly be noted that this movement was only suddenly set in motion by decision of the political power nearly ten years after the publication of *Dialectical and Historical Materialism*, more than fifteen years after the Stalinist interpretation of Marxist philosophy had been officially endorsed (by Mitin in 1932). If, as I have claimed, 'epistemological voluntarism' is a 'conclusion' from these philosophical theses, how could there be such a long interval between their formulation and its appearance? Moreover, how can this hypothesis explain why, despite the pressures exerted on them, Party and Government refused until 1948 to back Lysenko's doctrine and its philosophical presuppositions, while in other respects approving his agronomic techniques?

This question would be a decisive objection if the 'logic' of a philosophical argument were of the same kind as that of a scientific proof; if the necessity of its 'conclusions' conformed to an *internal* determination of its conceptual apparatus. But this is not the case: the organization of the theses of a given philosophy may also be governed by a 'logic' of its own, but it only develops its effects as a function of *something at stake* outside the play of its categories, determined by the social practice in which this philosophy occupies a position: this explains why a *single* philosophical apparatus may draw out all the effects of its theses, but also why one or other of its implications may be 'suspended', one or other of its positions temporarily or permanently 'neutralized', or why the philosophical charge may be displaced or condensed on to one or other of its theses at the expense of the others. . . .[16]

In the case which concerns us, the ontological version of dialectical materialism, the extreme implication of which, as we have seen, is the theory of the two sciences, can also, given the right conjuncture, function only in a minor mode, or simultaneously in a minor mode: 'suspending' the epistemological voluntarism it contains, neutralizing, i.e., camouflaging the normative character of the conception of the 'laws' of dialectics. We all know the drab scholasticism that then results: all too many works by 'Marxist' philosophers set out to discover in the various sciences, after the event, 'applications' of dialectical materialism; 'applications' which, given their external and *a posteriori* relation to the science, now have the peculiarity that they in no way change their 'object'. Such was the practice deduced before 1948 from the Stalinist version of dialectical materialism. It is also, it must be said, the one rediscovered with lazy and conformist relief by the majority of Marxist philosophers after the end of the Lysenkoist misadventure. . . .

These Marxist philosophers may well display all the outward marks of the most scrupulous respect for scientific work, in a manner which would not be disavowed by the most convinced positivist, but their philosophical enterprise is nonetheless still marked with the 'normativity' implied by their conception of dialectics. Their language alone is enough to prove it and to arouse the suspicions of practitioners of the science if they were not already alerted; every scientific discovery is celebrated – i.e. buried – solely as a 'confirmation' of dialectical materialism, if not as a 'brilliant illustration' of a 'prediction' of Engels or Lenin. . . .[17]

[16] The history of philosophy provides hundreds of examples of such a 'play' within the framework of a basic apparatus. For example, the 'play' of the minor Cartesians with respect to Descartes' apparatus, that of the post-Kantians with respect to Kant's, that of the neo-Hegelians with respect to Hegel. . . .

[17] I have already signalled (*Une Crise et son enjeu*, François Maspero, Paris 1973, p. 101n.) the monstrous *tour de force* performed by Bonifatii Kedrov, who undertakes (*Recherches Internationales*, 1971, Nos. 65–6, p. 32), without irony, to 'prove' that Lenin foresaw the results . . . of Mendelist genetics: 'When the enemies of genetics treated the recognition of the specific material supports of heredity as idealism and mysticism they were openly attacking the geneticist biologists, but they also went against principles that Lenin had laid down as the basis for the whole problem, i.e., that the difference between matter deprived of this determinate biological property (sensitivity) and matter endowed with it

This aberrant practice of Marxist philosophy amounts, according to the 'classical' device of idealist philosophies, to a real misappropriation of the sciences to the glory of a determinate philosophy – the state philosophy in the Soviet Union and the Eastern countries.

Just as evolutionism is merely the 'poor man's Hegelianism' (Althusser), this drab scholasticism is, beneath its modest positivist exterior, merely the poor man's voluntarism: a mere conformist tailism of the Stalinist voluntarist philosophy triumphally 'applied' in 1948. In philosophy, misery and triumph always share the same skin.

⋆   ⋆   ⋆

So what happened in 1948 to make dialectical materialism swing irreversibly to its 'voluntarist' variant in the official consecration of Lysenkoism?[18]

As we have seen, a formidable propaganda campaign was then mounted, propelled and generalized by the state apparatus. And on this occasion the campaign was deliberately and openly con-

---

lies solely in the mode of organization of the matter, i.e., in the difference between the bonds established between the same particles of matter (atoms, electrons).'

In a special number of *Recherches Internationales* recently devoted to 'Philosophical Studies in the Socialist Countries' (1975, No. 82), *all* the articles in which are deeply marked by the positivist variant of the ontological conception of dialectical materialism, there is one by Il'in and Frolov called 'Scientific Research and the Philosophical Confrontation in Biology' which manages to avoid even mentioning Lysenko's name and opens with a quotation from Engels's *Dialectics of Nature* which the contemporary development of biology is supposed to illustrate. . . . The reader will be able to judge for him or herself as to the effectiveness of such texts in the ideological battle.

[18] The event was seen as a sudden turn: as late as December 1947, Mitin, who can be regarded as having been Stalin's spokesman in philosophy since 1931, stuck to the idea of a compromise: while condemning the attacks on Lysenko, he flatly refused to denounce Mendelist genetics as a bourgeois pseudo-science as the Lysenkoists demanded. But six months later the same Mitin intervened during the discussion at the Academy of Agricultural Sciences to state: 'The methodology of the Michurin trend is based on the principles of dialectical materialism; it constructively develops Darwin's theory of evolution. . . . The Mendelist-Morganist trend in biology, on the contrary, is continuing and developing the thoroughly idealistic and metaphysical theory of Weismann. . . . No matter what reservations concerning Weismann's theory the representatives of the Mendel-Morgan trend in this country may attach to their statements, in substance, their theoretical foundation, their theoretical point of departure, is Weismannism, that reactionary and utterly bankrupt theory which denies that man can actively influence directed alteration of plant and animal organisms' (*Verbatim Report*, op. cit., p. 263). In short, Mitin had rallied completely to Lysenko's position on the theory of heredity.

What had happened?

ducted under the banner of the theory of the 'two sciences': it seized on Lysenko's doctrine, transforming it into a state doctrine and celebrating it as *the* illustration of the superiority of the Soviet regime over capitalist regimes in the domain of science and culture.

As we know, the fate of 'classical' genetics was thereby determined: a 'bourgeois science' objectively representing the interests of imperialism, it could not continue to exist in the 'land of socialism'. As we also know, it was on the same arguments that intellectuals outside the socialist camp were to be summoned to support Lysenko and that it was to become a political duty for Communists in all countries to defend and disseminate the Michurinist theory and the thesis of the 'two sciences'.

Under these conditions it is hardly surprising that Lysenko's name has remained linked to this alternative ('bourgeois science' *or* 'proletarian science') and that for many people, especially outside the USSR, but in the USSR too (as far as I can tell), Lysenkoism can be *reduced* to an amalgam of scientific charlatanism and state imposture. Only the epistemological monstrosities and the arbitrary intervention of the authorities have been remembered, the former have been seen as the effects of the latter, and the inopportune measures of a state which violated the freedom of scientific research denounced.[19] In other words, Lysenkoism has nearly always been treated in terms of truth and error, and the origin of their reversal has been sought in the intervention of the authorities legislating, as if it had that 'right', in matters of philosophy and scientific research. Hence the general indignation.

I do not dispute that this reduction is comprehensible as an immediate reaction to the *fait accompli* of the propaganda launched in 1948. Indignation, like rebellion, is also a political 'virtue'. But it should now be clear that this reduction is not enough to explain the real history of Lysenkoism. That real history cannot be conceived solely in terms of truth and error, i.e., in terms of a mere result subjected to a mere scientific judgement. The history of an ideological formation, even when it manipulates certain scientific concepts, is of another order of complexity. We have seen in fact that the history of Lysenkoism is that of a quite unique ideological

---

[19] This is the interpretation given by Vincent Labeyrie, for example, in *La Recherche*, April 1972. In essentials his argument amounted to a demonstration, against Jacques Monod, that the problem posed by the Lysenko affair was the universal problem of the 'objectivity of the organs responsible for the financing of research'.

formation which, like every ideological formation, had a material basis from the start. And this was the case with the first Lysenko providing a few precious recipes to Soviet agronomy. Even when the first techniques were 'seized' by theory (that of the phasic development of plants), they continued to play their part in the insertion of Lysenkoism into its social basis in the countryside where it served the Stalinist 'political line' of the 'technical' development of the productive forces. When dialectical materialism, in its Stalinist version, came to take over Lysenkoist theory, things began to change: yet it remained the case that it was on the dual basis of positions conquered in practice and of state intervention that the 'delirium' was to begin and grow, culminating in the official consecration in 1948.

Thus for a long time Lysenkoism can be seen as the condensation into a unified system of a consistent set of 'answers' given to a series of serious problems posed in social practice in the Soviet Union since the October Revolution, problems which were not scientifically mastered (for a variety of reasons, some scientific, some political).[20] Thus if one wants to explain the whole complex process in which empiricism sustained arbitrary theoretical propositions and the state intervened with varying objectives, one cannot pronounce in terms of error and truth.

On the other hand, it is legitimate to denounce the state's intervention, imposing the thesis of the 'two sciences'. For just as we have seen dialectical materialism seize on Lysenko's theory from outside, so we see the state intervene from outside to impose the ideology of the 'two sciences' on Lysenkoism and extend that ideology far beyond it. This was a new phenomenon. And it is very important to make it clear that it was for no reason *inside* Lysenko's theory that it attained its universal destiny in 1948. In

[20] The reader will already have noted that this analysis of Lysenkoism as a 'Stalinist phenomenon' contradicts the axiom that Jean Elleinstein has made the starting-point for his interpretation of the history of the Soviet Union (*The Stalin Phenomenon*, Lawrence and Wishart, London 1976). Elleinstein claims that what is called 'Stalinism' is a set of incorrect answers given to questions which were always correctly posed. It is clear that this is wrong: on the contrary, it is *because they were incorrectly posed* that the questions received the answers they did. The effect (or should I say the aim?) of Elleinstein's axiom is to restrict the explanation of the Stalinist deviation to *superstructural* phenomena; the explanation I am proposing for Lysenkoism – apparently a phenomenon strictly confined to the superstructure – shows that in reality one has to refer in the last instance to the infrastructure if one hopes to cast light on its formation. Nor, incidentally, should a Marxist find this surprising.

particular, it would be illusory to see in what happened then no more than an unwinding of the implications of a philosophical 'logic' to yield the theme of the 'two sciences' as the extreme consequence of previously established and practised official philosophical positions.

I should like here to suggest that, even if the theory of the 'two sciences' was implicitly inscribed in the Stalinist interpretation of dialectical materialism, and even if, even more paradoxically, it was the essential conclusion of a philosophy whose peculiar mixture of technocracy and humanism has constantly obsessed the Soviet intelligentsia – the philosophy of A. A. Bogdanov – when the thesis of the 'two sciences' was adopted and promoted in 1947–8, *it was not, it was no longer, a philosophical matter.*[21]

---

[21] Bogdanov's philosophy, which contained more than the *empirio-monist* theses fought by Lenin, deserves a special study. Here I shall only note one essential point.

The theory of the 'two sciences' appeared in Bogdanov's work as one of the main conclusions from the general conception of history that constituted the keystone of his system of 'tectology' (the science of organization).

The history of human societies has, according to Bogdanov, always been governed by a principle of *organization*, i.e., in conformity with the biological sense of this sociological metaphor, by a principle of mutual complementarity in the relations between the whole and its parts. According to this theory, through the struggles and dramas of real history, organization has always been attempting to realize itself, so that the division of society into classes only features in it as a provisional accident, a temporary postponement, always already overcome in principle, in the line of an inwardly purposeful movement. Class societies – in particular bourgeois society – are thought as imperfect realizations or incomplete drafts of organization: organizations whose principle – disorganization or anarchy – betrays their own essence; they appear as unstable realizations, undermined from the first by the mute contradiction which will sweep them away.

The proletarian revolution which has to put an end to this contradiction (organization/disorganization) at once becomes a 'parousia', a manifestation of the originary essence of society in the actual presence of a new society, the triumphant coming of organization. As for the proletariat, the agent of this coming, far from being defined by its place in capitalist relations of production, it is conceived as the bearer – or incarnation – of a project already inscribed from the beginning in the most embryonic forms of association between men: its historical mission is to accomplish this project and thus all its reality is summed up in its being the instrument of this accomplishment.

Here it is of little consequence by what conceptual juggling Bogdanov 'managed' to reconcile this idealist philosophy of history with historical materialism. Lenin showed that the cost was theoretical inconsistencies made all the more serious by Bogdanov's claim to base Marxist materialist theses on his idealist philosophical positions. . . .

It should just be noted that the theory of the 'two sciences' is an integral part of this doctrine, via the idea of a proletarian science yet to be created.

Indeed, it is clear that this theory follows 'logically' from the speculative construction outlined above: the proletariat, agent of social reorganization, has, among other tasks, that of 'reorganizing ideas' on a new basis and constructing a 'science of a new type' which will be adequate to the new social organization. This 'proletarian science', explained Bogdanov,

I want to argue that, behind the mask of the *generalization* of Lysenkoism, proposed as ideology to all intellectual workers, order and register were being shifted. It was no longer a question of 'scientific' or 'philosophical' theory; in fact what was happening was the consecration of a *state ideological system*: a state ideology in which the 'theory' of the two sciences is the crucial component – at once privileged instrument, functional model and theoretical 'touchstone'.

In short, we can say of the final avatar of Lysenkoism, the one in which it found its final form and status, what we have said about the earlier ones: that an event seized on it *from the outside* to assign it a role in the Soviet social formation.

Or else, if we wish to give these remarks the spice of paradox,

---

will be different by *nature* from bourgeois science because, resting on a non-contradictory material basis, it will open up unbounded horizons to human knowledge. . . .

Thus he could write: 'To say that the class character of science resides in the *defence of the interests* of a given class is only a pamphleteer's argument or a falsification pure and simple. In reality, science may be bourgeois or proletarian by its very "nature", notably in *its origins, its conceptions, its methods of study and exposition*. In this fundamental sense, all the sciences, including mathematics and logic, can have and really do have a class character.' The mission of the proletariat in this domain followed immediately: to proceed 'to the critical re-examination of all the sciences' which are in essential 'bourgeois', to the constitution of new disciplines and the elaboration of an Encyclopaedia modelled on Diderot's (bourgeois) Encyclopaedia.

But this is the decisive point: inverting the *technocratic* tendency to which he was pushed by the ambiguous theme of organization and which led him to describe socialism as the rationalization, centralization and planning of labour, Bogdanov went in another direction where *ideology* was concerned. When he had to describe the revolution which would be produced by the proletariat's accession to power, the same theme of organization led him to the utopian celebration of the appearance of a 'new type of humanity': all human relations, he explained, will be called to be 'reorganized' on the basis of the new relations of production. The very essence of the human species would, he argued, have to be changed in the process.

Thus Bogdanov's historical evolutionism presented the spectacle of culminating in a '*voluntarist humanism*' of political and ideological practice. And it is precisely because it was inscribed in this general perspective that the theory of the 'two sciences' was one of the essential arguments of Bogdanovist propaganda even before 1905 (from the moment he founded, with Gorkii, Lunacharskii and several others, the first workers' schools in Capri and Bologna). 'Proletarian science', a science of a 'new type', was to be the science of the 'new man'.

I have called this 'voluntarist humanism' to suggest that it is a 'humanism', since the aims of the revolution (and hence of history) are subordinate in it to a notion of the human essence; but also to mark the specific nuance which distinguishes this variant of humanism from its classical bourgeois forms – and their supposedly Marxist echoes – since here it is not a question of the reappropriation by man of an essence that has been lost – in 'Marxist' terminology, alienated – during the historical process, but rather one of the very *creation* of a new and as yet unknown human essence (see Appendix).

we can say that the 1948 Session only officially consecrated the success of Lysenko's theories – brushing aside all the objections and taking all the risks – because *it was no longer a question either of Lysenko or of his theories* but of something quite different which had constantly been practised previously in partial forms and finally achieved its general and systematic form at that date: a declared, obligatory state ideology which imposed on all intellectuals the Stalinist version of dialectical materialism beneath the rule of the supposed antagonism of 'bourgeois science' and 'proletarian science'.

★　　　★　　　★

Hence to explain the 1948 consecration is also to clarify the constitution of this state ideological system, to inquire into the mechanism by which it functioned and the reasons for its triumph.

Now it is clear that this ideology was not strictly speaking a mass ideology, not one addressed to the masses of the people: it was an ideology addressed to a definite social stratum, that of the intellectuals existing as a *distinct* social stratum, distinct because it was socially differentiated, not just by the intact if not reinforced division between manual and intellectual labour, but also by its status and social and material advantages. An idea of the composition of this social stratum can be obtained from what we have glimpsed of Lysenko's 'clientele' in the 1930's: it included not just scientists, researchers and intellectual workers in the different scientific and literary disciplines, but all those responsible for the intervention of science and its applications in production, managers and experts in the industrial and agricultural production units, experimental and machine units, to which should of course be added all cadres in the Party and the state apparatuses, who were intellectuals.

Thus this state ideology was aimed at that very important social stratum designated by the Russian term 'intelligentsia', which groups together all those who have economic, social, political and ideological responsibilities in the existence of the Soviet state – a social stratum (some have called it a social class) which has organic relations with the Party and state from which it draws its material privileges and its power; and on which in turn Party and state depend for the maintenance of their domination over the mass of workers and peasants.

But we must go further, because it is not enough to say that this ideology 'was addressed' to this social stratum or 'aimed' at it: it must be added that it was *imposed* on it in modalities that throw a vivid light on one of the most enigmatic aspects of Stalinist practice.

The facts here can serve as indices.

In 1948, under cover of the 'Cold War', the Party and the government announced that a class struggle of unprecedented intensity had begun in the Soviet Union and they made it obligatory on all intellectuals to conduct this struggle to the total victory of the proletarian point of view in all branches of learning and culture.

Class struggle: twelve years after 1936, when it was proclaimed and inscribed in the very Constitution that in the USSR the class struggle had . . . *disappeared!* Thus a country where Stalin claimed the class struggle had been surpassed and was therefore absent – where it was agreed that it had withered away during the 'construction of socialism' – saw continuously from 1935 and strikingly in 1948 the proclamation of an ideology formulated in terms of class struggle which did not hesitate to express itself in the extremism of a military vocabulary!

In other words, the class struggle, banished from the infrastructure (no more economic class struggle, no more social conflicts, no more strikes, etc.), banished from politics (no more parties other than the Communist Party, class enemies banished or shot), had thus taken refuge in pure ideology alone: science, letters, the arts and philosophy!

From this contradiction: the class struggle has disappeared in the USSR but the class struggle must be unleashed among the intellectuals, it seems to me that only one conclusion can be drawn: i.e., that there really was class struggle somewhere (and the deportations, imprisonments and mass murders are also proof of this, not to speak of the constantly re-emerging 'economic' difficulties), but in order to deal with it it was *decided* that it must take place among the intellectuals where it should be pursued to the bitter end, by all possible means. Behind this operation it is easy to discern both the complete conjuring away of the real class struggle and its transposition into a restricted social stratum: that of the 'intellectuals'.

*   *   *

But this is not all: the formulation of this supposed class struggle among the intellectuals took a form which must seem very strange to anyone with a minimum of Marxist culture. Knowing to what extent Marx and Engels, Lenin and Gramsci, not to speak of Mao, too, have insisted on the extreme complexity of the class struggle in ideology, not just on the complexity of its necessary relationship with material class conditions, but also on the complexity of its internal contradictions, one cannot but be stupefied by the crude and definitive schematism of the opposition between 'bourgeois science' and 'proletarian science'. Not only is this formula crude, it is also peremptory; not only does it, literally speaking, have no meaning, but what is infinitely more serious, it *imposes* one which is not really a meaning but rather an injunction.

This injunction is not difficult to decipher, knowing that it was addressed to intellectuals, and not forgetting that the term included all Party and state cadres as well as scientists, production experts and other higher technicians. The formula summed up the injunction imposed on them to join one camp or the other: either the camp of proletarian science (i.e., of the authorities) or the camp of bourgeois science (i.e., of the enemies of the authorities). And at the same time this injunction was a *warning*: either one camp or the other; he who is not with the authorities is against them, there is no third camp.[22] Thus at the same time the warning was a solemn *threat*. He who has not understood that he has to choose, and to choose to submit, will be treated as what he is: an enemy of the state and the Party.

An ideology of blackmail, intimidation and, eventually, repression, such was the terrible practical effect of this generalized formula of the 'two sciences' which only aped the class struggle the better to impose the reign of repression and, by means of this repression, to mobilize 'intellectuals' in the interests of the state's domination – and of their own domination – over the masses of the people: such is the kernel of the state ideological system which seized on Lysenkoism in 1948 to impose it on all intellectuals, with the academic ceremonial we have witnessed.

It will be said that it is strange to argue *simultaneously* that a social stratum had been formed which, because it had secured, then maintained the dictatorship of the state apparatus over the masses

[22] The pseudo-third camp was the one then denounced, especially in the genetics debate, as that of 'cosmopolitanism' and bourgeois 'objectivism'.

of the people, drew from it material advantages which ensured its solidarity with and dependence on the authorities, and also that this same social stratum had had *imposed* on it (to tell the truth, over a long period, during which the argument had received a high polish) as its own ideology an ideology of injunction, warning and threat. For as we know, at the end of this ideology were the trials and the camps, torture and deaths from exhaustion, hunger and ill-treatment. Thus it will be asked, how could a social stratum have allowed such an ideology, trapping it in a fatal alternative, to be imposed on it and even accept it, i.e., *practise it itself?*

Yet this is precisely what happened; and what is even more astonishing, this ideology managed to work in this way by the well regulated 'play' of its internal organization.

I am obviously not so thoughtless as to suppose that such an ideology could have worked by virtue of its 'ideas' alone. If it is true that all ideology exists in its practices and that its practices can be those of a state apparatus (Althusser), then this cynical ideology did not have to look far for its practices and its apparatus: it found them on the spot in the state police, the emergency tribunals, the prisons, the expeditive measures, the trials, the executions and the camps. Thus this terribly practical threat, used every day, was the first precondition for the victory and then maintenance of this ideology.

But what I am trying to draw attention to is the fact that, thus sustained by this apparatus of terror, the ideology of the 'two sciences' (which obviously had effects far outside the unfortunate sciences alone . . .) had *in its form* the wherewithal to work *by itself* as well. As it enjoined on every intellectual the ineluctable destiny of occupying either the place of the authorities or the place of the enemy (and hence that of the victim), and as, in the implacable abstraction of the terms that designated them, neither of the two places was the object of an objective, fixed definition, no one could ever be certain in advance (experience proved this for numerous cadres, not just in the police, but also in politics) that they were in the safe place. They could only gain this certainty by rallying to the official positions of the day and changing when they changed (just one example: Mitin). But in this way they helped to strengthen both their servitude and the ideology in which they had to find their place, constantly exposed as they were to the risk of being caught in the trap of their conformism, since these positions were changing.

Everything we know about the Stalinist prison system (and the great trials) proves that with few exceptions, it was diabolically successful in making its prisoners accept their own captivity, its martyrs their own 'guilt'. At its own level, the ideology of the 'two sciences', as a complement to this repression, worked along the same lines: it was so constituted that it was fuelled by the verbal consent and practical conformism of those enjoined to submit to it.[23] And, like the convicts and dying who could preserve some excuse for Stalin in their hearts during their agony, the intellectuals condemned to the dilemma of the two sciences and the practices of represssion were able to find the sinister consolation of thinking that they were participating in the 'class struggle' nonetheless: the ideology of the two sciences thus cemented their unity in power as well as in servitude and death.

* * *

It will be argued that these are no more than indications, and indices. I agree. It will be argued that they do not explain the whole social situation of the USSR, its social and political conflicts and the causes that finally produced a gigantic dictatorship of a state apparatus fused with the Party under the slogans of Marxism-Leninism. Of course. It will be argued that the ideology of the 'two sciences' was only valid for the intellectuals and not for the masses of the people,

[23] Reread the statements of 'self-criticism' by three of the most noteworthy Mendelists at the end of the 1948 Session. They are all the more poignant in that the contrast with their previous speeches is accentuated by the temporal proximity (two days!). They illustrate, if that is the word, the incredible power of the ideological mechanism I am describing.

Here is Zhukovskii:

'The speech I made the day before yesterday, at a time when the Central Committee of the Party had drawn a dividing line between the two trends in biological science, was unworthy of a member of the Communist Party and of a Soviet scientist. I admit that the position I held was wrong. Academician Lobanov's noteworthy speech yesterday, and I esteem P. P. Lobanov as a fine statesman, his words directly addressed to me – our ways must part – moved me deeply. His speech agitated me profoundly. A sleepless night helped me to think over my behaviour. Academician Vasilenko's speech also made a deep impression upon me, for he showed how closely the Michurinists are connected with the people, and how important it is at this juncture to cherish the prestige of our President. The exceptional unity displayed by the members and guests at this Session, the demonstration of the power of this unity and the bonds with the people, and, on the contrary, the demonstration of the weakness of the opponents are to me so obvious, that I declare that I shall fight – and there are times when I can fight – for the Michurinian biological science. (Prolonged applause)' (*Verbatim Report*, op. cit., p. 618).

The interventions of Alikhanyan and Polyakov reproduced the same terms.

to whom Stalin spoke simultaneously in a *different* language, that of the construction of socialism, the coming of the 'new man', the mobilization against imperialism, etc., meanwhile imposing on them the practice of mass repression. I completely agree. But I am taking the few elements at our disposal from a history the sources of which are deliberately closed, from a history completely mute about itself, in order to obtain from them as much light as possible and to cast it on the ideology of the 'two sciences' which presided over Lysenko's triumph in 1948. And it seems to me that by restricting its use to intellectuals as I have done and situating this social stratum on the side of the power whose instrument it was, it becomes possible to understand the effects the Soviet authorities, with Stalin at their head, drew from it. This social stratum that they held by material privileges and the power they granted it, they subjected ideologically to themselves in the name of an imaginary class struggle between the two sciences. And the logic of this ideology was such that no one could disavow it without ranking themselves in the category of enemies of the authorities, hence in a place inscribed in advance in this ideology opening directly onto repression. It was an infernal circle in that it could not be exercized without confirming and reinforcing itself, allowing no other initiative to individuals than the enthusiasm of conformism or the banality of commentary – in all cases servitude. Through this ideology those who participated in the power of the authorities and its privileges were at the mercy of the authorities they served from the start. . . .

The reasons for the victory of Lysenkoism in 1948 were also reasons why it should last: they also explain the incredible resistance it subsequently put up against its opponents and . . . against practical disproofs.

6

In Memoriam

From 1948 to 1952, Lysenko's power was absolute: none of his decisions was disputed any longer, none of his theses criticized. Every hostile publication was banned. He undertook to reorganize biology teaching from top to bottom, imposed new textbooks and 'retrained' teachers. There was a systematic purge of the various biological institutes under the umbrella of the Academy of Sciences. As for the Mendelists, their laboratories were confiscated; they were denied the right to pursue their teaching and their research.

But Lysenkoism did not depend for its fate on academic educational institutions. Agricultural technicians had made Lysenko's fortune; he had achieved his fame on the basis of a few spectacular successes obtained in agronomy; he had been able to face up to all his critics and defeat the Mendelist geneticists thanks to the favour his theories enjoyed in the experimental stations. And it was also here that the test of time led to his decline: when the more fantastic applications of the new theory of heredity had ended in spectacular failures that could no longer be concealed.

In 1952 a series of setbacks amounting to a minor disaster in this area made decisive inroads into Lysenko's power. These failures occurred in the implementation of what was then called the 'Great Plan for the Transformation of Nature' or the 'October 20th Plan', laid down in its broad lines by Stalin as a combination of the theses of Vil'yams and Lysenko.

Here are the terms in which Francis Cohen described this plan in *L'Europe* no. 39, March 1949, under the symptomatic title 'The Golden Age: Objective No. 1 in the USSR': 'The Bolshevik Party and the Soviet Government, basing themselves on the experience of scientists and collective-farm workers, have drawn up the "October 20th Plan", whose implementation should in fifteen years transform the steppe into a veritable park extending over an area of 120 million hectares – twice the area of France. The first point of the plan is to plant a network of windbreaks and forest shelterbelts. These trees will stop the winds, hold in moisture, prevent the snow from melting too quickly and force it to feed the ground with water, suppress surface drainage and hence destructive erosion. Eight main belts will be planted by the state. One, following the Ural River, will stretch from the Caspian Sea to the Ural Mountains. Three others, along the Volga, on the East and the West of the great river, form a second and third barrier. Along the Don, the Donets and between the Don and the Volga, the last four belts will complete the system: in all 5,300 kms in length (about the perimeter of France) and 540,000 hectares in area (about one hundred times the area of the Forest of Fontainebleau).

'At the same time, the state farms and collective farms will plant windbreaks on their lands of a ten times larger total area: 5,700,000 ha. The banks of watercourses will be planted with trees; the slopes of ravines, the edges of ponds will be wooded, the sands of the Caspian region will be fixed. Each "break", i.e., each field containing the same crop, will be separated from its neighbours by trees' (pp. 100–101). The plan included many other measures of the same kind and noted that all this could only be realized by the use of Lysenkoist methods (cluster planting) and Lysenkoist seeds.

It was customary to celebrate this plan as a 'grandiose' initiative. It is clear that this was no exaggeration.

By 1952 the failures had become so significant as to make the Ministry of Agriculture send new directives on shelterbelts which implicitly abandoned the Lysenkoist method of cluster planting of trees.[1] Even before Stalin's death in March 1953, the implementation of the 'Grand Plan' had in fact been abandoned in the form in which it had been announced.

Simultaneously, in 1952, the 'Mendelist' geneticists initiated a counter-attack, based on the failures in practice of the Lysenkoist methods. They began to turn against Lysenko the arguments of effectiveness he had used against them in 1948. One journal provided them with a rallying point: the *Botanicheskii Zhurnal* (*Botanical Journal*). Medvedev well describes the episodes in this campaign, which culminated in 1955 in Lysenko's resignation as

---

[1] Joravsky, op. cit., p. 154.

President of the Academy of Agricultural Sciences and his replacement by Lobanov.

But the essential point is that after 1952, experts and cadres in agricultural production – the backbone of the Lysenkoist troops – began to lose confidence in Lysenko: the crucial element of his strength was thus slipping away. We possess only clues to this withdrawal, but they are irrefutable. The first is a speech to the 19th Party Congress on behalf of the Central Committee by Malenkov in October 1952, which spoke for cadres in agriculture and plainly stated that although 'all anti-scientific, reactionary ideas have been exposed and destroyed in agricultural science, and it is developing now on the only correct, materialist, Michurinist basis . . ., nevertheless it is still lagging behind the requirements of production on the collective and state farms' (cit. Joravsky, op. cit., p. 155). The second is Lysenko's own recriminations; from 1953 on, he constantly complained, with the support of concrete examples, that his directives were only being applied incompletely, slowly and without enthusiasm.

The fact that this retreat was gradual and even very slow is easily explained along the lines of the preceding analyses: Lysenkoism had been organically linked to the political line followed by the Party in agricultural matters for twenty years; precisely to the line which had 'produced' the social stratum of experts, managers and cadres for which Lysenkoist theory had provided an ideological cement.

So there is nothing surprising in the fact that Stalin's death did not lead to Lysenko's fall: only those who see Lysenko as an emanation of Stalin's 'madness' or of the 'cult of personality' and ignore the real historical and social roots of Lysenkoism can find it disconcerting.

Moreover, the situation was complicated by the fact that in 1948 those with ideological and political responsibility in the Party had publicly and unreservedly committed themselves to Lysenko and applied to his doctrine the label 'dialectical materialism'. Hence, without a general re-examination of the question of Lysenkoism, which must have led to an interrogation not only of the nature of Marxist philosophy and its practice in the preceding years, but also that of the question of the forms of ideological struggle and agricultural policy overall since 1917; hence a re-examination which would be inseparable from a critical analysis of all the problems posed by the 'construction of socialism' in the USSR, it was not possible to 'drop' Lysenko.

As we know, this great re-examination never occurred; so Lysenko still had to be supported. Given the repeated attacks made on him, the authorities had to commit themselves in his favour once again: on September 29th 1958, *Pravda* announced the award of the Order of Lenin to Lysenko and unreservedly praised his work and doctrine. In December of the same year, a plenary session of the Central Committee of the Party was convened which solemnly reiterated its confidence in Lysenko, reaffirmed its approval for the methods and theories of Michurinist biology and firmly invited Lysenko's opponents to stop their attacks. The editorial board of the *Botanicheskii Zhurnal* were removed and a Lysenkoist team took it over.

For all that, Lysenkoist techniques of selection were being abandoned in practice at the same time. And as a culminating paradox, in consequence of the great revolution which genetics had undergone since the work of Watson and Crick on the structure of DNA and which was beginning to make 'applications' of it actually possible and effective in agriculture, Lysenko's methods were tending to be replaced by openly 'Mendelist' techniques.

Khrushchev's political astuteness is demonstrated by his understanding that there was only one way out of this untenable situation: to get Lysenko to adopt officially agricultural programmes which no longer had anything essential to do with Lysenkoism. Joravsky correctly notes that the famous campaign organized by Khrushchev for the massive planting of maize was based on the use of 'heterosis', a Mendelist method that Lysenko had expressly fought for many years. . . .[2]

Lysenko lent himself to this device with astonishing compliance considering the dogmatic arguments he had previously put forward in favour of his positions: he was rewarded in 1961 when he was restored to the Presidency of the Academy of Agricultural Sciences.

However, it was more and more urgently necessary every day that teaching and research in 'classical' genetics be officially restored. But here too appearances had to be kept up. This was the double

---

[2] A method which consists, by means of polyploidy, of exploiting hybrid vigour in cases of quantitative characters in order to increase yields. The average increase obtained by this method for maize has been estimated at 37%.

imperative to which the decisions taken by the Central Committee and the Council of Ministers in June 1963 were a response: while emphasizing the interest of Michurinist biology, in fact they restored the compromise situation of before 1948, since they encouraged '*all*' research in biology, medicine and the agronomic sciences.

Medvedev's book provides a detailed account of the battle then joined about this decree. Each of the tendencies attempted to exploit it to its own advantage. The important thing, however, is that the process of the re-establishment of genetics was irreversibly under way.

Khrushchev had personally committed himself to Lysenko on several further occasions. Khrushchev's 'resignation' provided the opportunity for forcing Lysenko's retirement at the beginning of 1965.

As the result of a meeting of the Academy of Sciences, he had to leave his post as Director of the Institute of Genetics. At the same time, commissions began to work out new biology textbooks and to organize courses for teachers to bring them up to date with the latest developments of genetics in the West.

The official end of Lysenkoism was occasioned by a symbolic demonstration on the centenary of Mendel's *Memoir* (1865), celebrated with great pomp at Brno in the presence of a large Soviet delegation composed of the most noteworthy of those who had been Lysenko's opponents in 1948. . . .

$$*\qquad*\qquad*$$

On October 10th 1975, *Le Monde* reported on the solemn session of the USSR Academy of Sciences in celebration of its 250th anniversary. The report contained the following lines:

'The Academicians, numbering 245, are elected by secret ballot, which is by no means usual here. More astonishing, Academicians are elected for life and cannot be removed from their work except by a decision of the Presidium of the Academy. Of course, there are a few exceptions to this rule: the most noteworthy was that of Molotov, the former Minister for Foreign Affairs, condemned by Khrushchev in 1957 for anti-Party activities, and expelled from the Academy. On the other hand, Andrei Sakharov is still a member. So, moreover, is Tromfim Denisovich Lysenko, the "charlatan" of genetics, even though he fell into disgrace at the same time as his protector, Mr. "K". Lysenko, who succeeded in getting his absurd theory of the existence of a bourgeois genetics and a proletarian genetics proclaimed as dogma, was also a participant at the Session in the Palace of Congresses.'

A few days later, a speech by the Minister of Agriculture involuntarily revealed the catastrophic figures for cereal production in 1974.

The concatenation of these two facts alone illustrates what I hope has been one of the main lessons of this essay in historical analysis: a politics that retreats from the criticism of its own errors remains willy-nilly subject to the effects of their causes.

Appendix

Bogdanov, Mirror of the Soviet Intelligentsia*

1 Lenin versus Bogdanov

If one were to speculate as to the reasons for the oblivion into which the works of Aleksandr Bogdanov have fallen for more than half a century, the first that comes to mind seems to provide a sufficient explanation on its own: on two occasions, ten years apart, Bogdanov was theoretically and politically condemned by Lenin. An uncompromising refutation of his philosophical theses in *Materialism and Empirio-criticism* (1909) and a vigorous struggle against the 'ultra-left' political positions of that fraction of the Bolshevik Party (the 'Otzovists') which had formed around him in the reflux following the unsuccessful revolution of 1905; then a number of lapidary criticisms of the notion of 'proletarian culture' (1920) which Bogdanov had adopted as the emblem for his theoretical and political work, and, finally, political opposition to the forms of organization of the Proletkult, the cultural mass movement inspired by Bogdanovism which embraced many revolutionary intellectuals, Bolshevik or otherwise, in Russia after the October Revolution.

So it is hardly surprising that Bogdanov's *oeuvre* should have joined so many others in the hell of Soviet libraries and not re-emerged to this day; that very soon all that was known of Bogdanov's writings became the few quotations from them produced for refutation by Lenin and Plekhanov; and that Bogdanov's name was assigned, along with other more famous ones, to the arsenal of incriminating epithets which provided ammunition for the

---

* This appendix appeared in French as an introduction to a selection of Bogdanov's writings entitled *La Science, l'art et la classe ouvrière*, translated and annotated by Blanche Grinbaum, presented by Dominique Lecourt and Henri Deluy; published by François Maspero, Paris 1977. (Translator's note.)

Stalinist practice of ideological and political struggle. The Soviet state's permanent exaltation of an 'official' version of Leninism presented as a corpus of definitive answers to supposedly settled questions, i.e., as detached from the contradictions and torments of the real history during which Lenin's thought was actually hammered out and tested, could only assign one fate to a twice condemned opponent of Lenin's: that he be no longer read.

Thus the first, most immediate and obvious interest of a translation of some of Bogdanov's essential writings, is to restore to historians and philosophers a *document* which is indispensable both to the knowledge of a period in the history of the Bolshevik revolution (1905–20), the one that largely sealed its fate, and to the understanding of the Leninist practice of philosophy whose principles we are only now, after so many years, beginning to be able to extract from the dogmatic matrix in which they are held in the reigning version of dialectical materialism.

But these texts do not have only a documentary interest, for the remarkable persistence of the basic theoretical positions which Bogdanov defended from *Empirio-monism* (1904–6) to *Tectology* (1912–16) itself poses a question which has implications going far beyond the 'case' of the intellectual and political history of the prolific theoretician and indefatigable activist that Bogdanov was; a question which ultimately allows us to throw an unexpected light on to the theoretical and ideological bases of the 'Stalinist deviation'. This question is that of the resistance of the Bogdanovist themes to Lenin's criticisms.

Anyone who has read *Materialism and Empirio-criticism* would be justified in thinking that Bogdanov could hardly survive such an onslaught and that his system, dismantled and denounced by Lenin as an eclectic assemblage of 'unspeakable nonsense' could be expected to have disappeared promptly from the theoretical stage of the Bolshevik revolution, or at least to have had to undergo profound reorganization in order to survive. In fact the opposite was the case: not only did the Bogdanov system, despite a progressive decentring of its main themes, continue to develop on its own terms, without apparently taking the slightest notice of the destructive refutation it had been subjected to, but in addition, Bogdanov reappeared at the centre of the political stage in the middle of the October Revolution as the inspiration and organizer of a movement infinitely more powerful than the tiny fraction of the 'Otzovists' had ever been, a genuine mass movement for a 'cultural revolution' which in three years was to reach several hundreds of thousands of people organized in the institutions of the Proletkult (workers' schools, libraries, proletarian theatres . . .).

The very fact demands explanation: how was it that, although he had been pulverized theoretically and defeated politically, Bogdanov's audience increased in the years following the publication of *Materialism and Empirio-criticism* and the dispute about boycotting the Duma?[1] But what is even odder is Lenin's attitude to this rise of Bogdanovism. When asked to take up a position towards Bogdanov's later productions, he was irritated and impatient. 'Bogdanov is not a Marxist,' he repeated in justification of the refusal to print any further articles by him in *Pravda*. 'Under the guise of "proletarian culture" A. A. Bogdanov is imparting bourgeois and reactionary views,' he noted drily in 1920 in the Preface to the Second Edition of *Materialism and Empirio-criticism*, alluding to *Tectology*, which he admitted he had not read. There followed the administrative measures which were a decisive blow for the Proletkult, subordinating it to the Commissariat for Education (Narkompros)[2] and finally driving Bogdanov out of political activity.[3] Clearly, Lenin did not understand the persistent favour 'Bogdanovism' found with Bolshevik intellectuals. He neglected to analyse its causes and attempted to counteract its effects by violent means, in sharp contrast to what was his constant practice in the treatment of ideological and theoretical differences: a practice of argument, which, although always conducted with passion, showed no reluctance to go into the minute details of the opponents' positions in order to convince.

I believe that one and the same reason, to be found plainly inscribed in Bogdanov's writings, will explain both the response to Bogdanov's theses and Lenin's unusual reaction, brutal in practice and summary in its theoretical justifications.

[1] As will be well-known, Bogdanov and his comrades drew from the defeat of 1905 the conclusion that nothing more was to be expected from legal action. They were therefore hostile to the Bolsheviks participating in the Duma (the Russian parliament). It was against this political position that Lenin intervened, and in order to destroy the theoretical foundations they claimed to have given it that he took up his pen against 'Mach's Russian disciples'.

[2] Lunacharskii, the 'God Builder' and former comrade of Bogdanov's, headed this Commissariat.

[3] Bogdanov returned to his profession as a doctor, founded the first Blood Transfusion Centre, and died in 1928 as a result of an experimental injection he had made on himself.

The reader of Bogdanov's texts cannot fail to note that in them the slogan of the construction of a 'proletarian culture' which gradually became the Bogdanovist theme *par excellence*, the key to his political career, is directly linked to an aspect of his doctrine already found in *Empirio-monism* but playing a larger and larger part in the later writings, to the point of becoming the unifying element of the final system of *Tectology*; an aspect in which Bogdanov believed and stated as early as 1904 that he had marked himself off from the positivist philosophy (the 'empirio-criticism' of the scientist Ernst Mach)[4] the essentials of whose conceptual apparatus he thought it necessary to take over for reasons relating to his idea of the theoretical conjuncture; an aspect of his doctrine which he held justified him in saying he was a Marxist, a claim he was never to renounce. This aspect is what I shall call a real *metaphysics of labour* as Absolute Origin of entities and thoughts which claimed to find its empirical guarantees in the imaginary 'facts' of a biologistic-evolutionistic ideology of *Organization*.[5]

The texts leave no doubt at all on this point: it is this metaphysics that unites the ideological themes and the political positions of Bogdanovism, at first sight spectacularly contradictory; 'ultra-left' themes – the best known – expressed and exalted in a mysticism of the modern industrial labourer, supporting 'ouvrierist' political positions of a sectarianism that is sometimes lyrical; themes that must be described as 'rightist' which appear in his theoretical edifice not just as the correlate but also as the foundation for the former and are reflected in a mysticism of machinery – of 'mechanized production'. A mysticism which in its turn justifies an openly technocratic conception of the socialist organization of production and a mechanistic theory of ideological transformations.

It is this metaphysics of labour and its implications that constitute the ultimate explanation for the extraordinary responsiveness of the Russian revolutionary intelligentsia to a theory so abstract and

[4] Later we shall see what it was in this philosophy, which Bogdanov described as 'the most rigorous form of positivism', that let him regard it as a scientific philosophy and one capable of being brought into concordance with Marxist philosophy.

[5] The system Bogdanov finally came up with was called 'tectology', meaning literally (and this is the sub-title of the book he devoted to it) 'universal science of organization'. The biological metaphor of Organization was not new in social theory: formed in the eighteenth century, Saint-Simon had adopted it, and Auguste Comte had made a systematic use of it, in a new sense, in the *Cours de philosophie positiviste*. A use which was to give rise to bourgeois sociology.

obscure that it was hardly predestined to popularity for any other reason. Bogdanov relayed to this intelligentsia, and they immediately and enthusiastically recognized themselves in it, a systematized representation of their own 'spontaneous' ideology, dignified by the authority of Marx. An ideology in which the ouvrierism was no more than the other side of a disappointed populism[6] giving these intellectuals the opportunity to express all their petty-bourgeois hostility to the peasantry; an ideology in which the 'technicism' was sustained by an idealist conception of the Revolution, descending in a straight line from the eighteenth century, as the advent of Reason.

Now, Lenin was very well aware of the danger represented in the political battle of Bogdanovism's 'ultra-left' positions. He did his utmost to combat what he correctly saw as the *anti-peasant* aspect of the slogan of 'proletarian culture'. The increasing difficulties of the years from 1918, which had a serious effect on the relations of the Party and the State with the peasantry, dictated to him that he put as rapid as possible a stop to this undertaking, which involved many Bolsheviks. Hence the brutal decision of 1920, which completely disoriented a number of well-meaning militants who could not make out the reasons for it.[7]

But on the other hand, if he did denounce the reactionary ideas conveyed by Bogdanov 'under the guise of proletarian culture', he gave no analysis as a basis for this diagnosis. Why? Obviously, the lack of time Lenin invokes in the preface to the second edition of *Materialism and Empirio-criticism* does not provide an adequate explanation. I shall interpret his evasion of an argued refutation of the later Bogdanov as implying quite simply that he did not have the theoretical means to carry it out. Or more precisely: that in the central matter of labour and its organization he shared with a whole generation of Bolsheviks some of the ideological presuppositions that Bogdanov systematized in his metaphysical theory.

Consider, for example, Lenin's conception of the organization of

---

[6] Bogdanov himself had started out as a populist, as he recalls himself in his text on the *Proletarian University*. In 1896 he left the Narodnaya Vol'ya movement to join the Social-Democrats. For biographical details, the reader should refer either to D. Grille's monograph *Lenins Rivale: Bogdanov und seine Philosophie*, Abhandlungen des Bundesinstituts für ostwissenschaftliche und internationale Studien, Band XII, Köln 1966, or to the biographical documents in *La Science, l'art et la classe ouvrière*, op. cit.

[7] See for example the contemporary article by A. Dodonova, translated into French in *Action poétique* no. 59.

labour in the units of production of modern industry under the dictatorship of the proletariat. As is well known, from 1918 on, Lenin demanded the systematic introduction of Taylorism in Russia. Robert Linhart has recently brilliantly demonstrated the short and long term implications of this position of Lenin's.[8] And he has shown that, based on an incorrect conception of the labour process, it presupposed that 'Taylorism can be dissociated from its function in capitalist exploitation' and seen solely as the constitution of a 'science of the organization of labour', socially neutral because it is purely rational, and hence applicable in any mode of production. In fact, contrasting this 'rational and reasoned distribution of labour inside the factory' with the anarchy reigning in capitalist society, Lenin came to consider it as a prototype of the rational overall organization of a socialist society.

Now, these positions, which imply a naturalist conception of technique as such and a technicist conception of the relations of production, are precisely, point by point and almost word for word, the positions held by Bogdanov in his 'universal science of organization'. Bogdanov, who, as we shall see, cites Taylorism as the type of a rational organization of labour and who was among the first to devote an article to the Taylor system, in 1913, celebrating it as the anticipation in a capitalist regime, as a result of the development of the productive forces, of what would tomorrow be the organization of socialist society. Bogdanov, who, at the same period, in two political science–fiction novels[9] presented a utopian picture of the future society as the Triumph of Reason in the form of the universal extension to all the spheres of social life of the system of the 'socialist rationalization' of production.

This explains Lenin's embarrassment in 1920, his irritation and his evasions in the face of the theoretical Bogdanovism of the Proletkult: even if he did remain radically hostile to Bogdanov's doctrine as such, for the reasons he had given in 1909, there is no doubt that there was a very profound concordance between some of his positions on the 'construction of socialism' which reveal the 'unperceived limits of his thought' (Linhart) and certain basic ideological themes theorized and popularized by Bogdanov.[10]

[8] See this genuinely Leninist book analysing the living contradictions of Lenin's thought, referring them to the concrete conjuncture it had to confront: *Lénine, les paysans, Taylor*, Editions du Seuil, Paris 1976.

[9] *Red Star* and *Engineer Menni*.

[10] In his book, Linhart correctly emphasizes the fact that this was not a unilaterally

The reader should make no mistake: the preceding remarks are not of interest just as a scholarly re-assessment of a point in the theoretical and political history of Leninism; as I have suggested, they make it possible to cast an unexpected light on the ideological and theoretical bases of the 'Stalinist deviation'. For the peculiar fate still in store for Bogdanovist themes in Soviet ideology is only explicable once they have been established.

It will be clear from my argument that these themes did not indeed vanish overnight with the end of the Proletkult, but, denounced rather than analysed and searchingly criticized by Lenin, they continued on the contrary to lead a subterranean life in Soviet ideology. To the extent that, paradoxically, the Bogdanovist system remained an inexhaustible reservoir for the verbally 'left-wing' themes of Stalinist propaganda in which they became constitutive elements. From the voluntarist humanism whose hymn to the 'new man' was intoned in 1935 and later, to become with Stakhanovism[11] the central motif in a grandiose mythology of the working class and technical progress, to the theory of the 'two sciences' which in 1948, at Zhdanov's instigation,[12] became a redoubtable weapon in the Party's hands to close the ranks of intellectuals around it in a moment of crisis . . . , all these themes are, as will be observed, present as such in Bogdanov's writings, whose unadmitted offspring they are.

In the last analysis, there is nothing surprising about this, insofar as, basically in accord with the economistic line adopted by the Bolshevik Party in and after 1928–30, they could easily be constituted as the utopian counterpoint that this line and the repressive practices that accompanied it needed for their implementation. And as these themes simply reflected the 'spontaneous' ideology of the Proletkultist intellectuals from whose ranks many cadres and

---

'technicist' position: Lenin expected that the application of 'rationalized' labour methods would have educational effects on a labour force whose origins were massively peasant and whose inexperience of factory work was having a seriously damaging effect on nascent Soviet industry.

[11] The Stakhanovites were initially, in the image of the miner Stakhanov, workers who had surpassed production norms and introduced technical improvements in machine industry; but they were soon also workers privileged by an appreciably higher than average wage, technical training and cadre functions in the organization of production.

[12] As is well known, it was A. Zhdanov who, on the publication on June 24th 1947 of the *History of Western Philosophy* edited by G. F. Aleksandrov, launched the movement of 'ideological struggle' which was to lead in the following year to the official adoption of Lysenko's 'agrobiological' theories and to affect all scientific, literary and artistic disciplines.

organizers of production and education were drawn,[13] they could continue silently as the ideological cement of their unity around the Party leadership. Stalin realized this and played on it to mobilize them in every period of tension that the Soviet Union traversed.

I opened by discussing the *oblivion* into which Bogdanov's works have fallen for half a century. It now takes on a new and deeper meaning: it is the oblivion of what is inadmissible about Soviet ideology, of the presence in its heart of what Lenin, without being able to deal with them fully, called 'bourgeois and reactionary views'.

It is this oblivion, and the relationship to the past which it contains, that it is now time to break.

We need to read Bogdanov.

2   Bogdanov's Philosophical Positions

After 1904, when the first part of *Empirio-monism* was published, all Bogdanov's work was organized on the basis of a fundamental philosophical armature which was never to be reconsidered. Thus a few basic theses were to remain characteristic of his philosophy. They are precisely the theses that Lenin attacked in *Materialism and Empirio-criticism*. They can all be summarized as borrowings from the then fashionable doctrine[14] of the German scientist Ernst Mach; a doctrine customarily designated as 'empirio-criticism', although Mach himself never used the term.

Mach's philosophy[15] was a scientist's philosophy: it was presented as a response, supposedly one based on scientific results obtained in psycho-physiology, to the 'state of crisis' which contemporary physics was then claimed to have entered as a result of the formulation of the second law of thermodynamics;[16] on this basis, it

[13] The case of A. Gastev, a Proletkultist put in charge of an institute of labour organization, is probably the most typical. Texts by Gastev can be found in French translation in *Action poétique* no. 59.

[14] In his book on *Dialectical Materialism* (Routledge and Kegan Paul, London 1958), Gustav Wetter emphasized that this fashion was the more influential in Russia in that, since the 1850's, many Russian intellectuals had followed the movement 'back to Kant' – and beyond Kant to Hume – which had influenced German philosophy in an anti-Hegelian direction, a movement which directly gave rise to Mach's doctrine.

[15] Robert S. Cohen has given an excellent systematic examination of Mach's philosophy, reproduced as 'Ernst Mach: Physics, Perception and the Philosophy of Science,' *Synthèse* no. 18, 1968, pp. 132–70; this article is followed by an appendix on Bogdanov. A good summary of the doctrine can be found in Leszek Kolakowski's *Positivist Philosophy from Hume to the Vienna Circle*, translated by N. Guterman, Penguin Books, Harmondsworth 1972.

[16] In my book *Une Crise et son enjeu, Essai sur la position de Lénine en philosophie* (collection 'Théorie', François Maspero, Paris 1973), I have tried to explain the constitution of this

developed a general theory of knowledge and of the history of the sciences. It thus vaunted itself as the first scientific philosophy ever produced, and proclaimed its ability to free the sciences from the illusions of metaphysics, to which it imputed the theoretical difficulties physics was undergoing.

Now, the main metaphysical illusion, according to Mach, was the philosophical distinction, uncritically accepted by most scientists, between matter and mind. It was this distinction that he claimed to be in a position to dismiss. The results of his work on the *Analysis of Sensations*,[17] he said, justified him in maintaining that every sensation is the result of a more or less complex combination of 'elements'[18] about which it would be vain to ask whether they are 'physical' or 'mental', if they belong to 'matter' or to 'mind', since they are, he claimed, 'neutral', prior to matter or to mind.

In this way, by presenting his philosophy as 'the philosophy of the contemporary sciences of nature', Mach could claim to have overcome to his own satisfaction the fundamental philosophical opposition between materialism and idealism: the question of the primacy of matter over thought, or of thought over matter, no longer arises, he claimed, once the common, indeterminate element that constitutes the ultimate horizon of all our knowledge has been registered.[19]

---

supposed 'state of crisis'. Since the 'classical' concept of matter, in harmony with the presuppositions of analytical mechanics, could not explain the *irreversible character* of thermodynamic phenomena, the openly idealist philosophical conclusion that 'matter had disappeared' was drawn, instead of noting, as Lenin suggested, that the scientific concept of matter was changing in form and working to establish its new determinations.

[17] Bogdanov wrote a preface for the Russian edition of the book with this title.

[18] The notion of the 'element', a key one in Mach's philosophy, referred to contemporary studies in 'psycho-physics' in which Mach himself had participated. He believed that the scientific authority of the works of Helmholtz could be adduced in its favour, for the latter, in his famous studies of acoustic phenomena, had decomposed musical sounds into their ultimate 'elements'. Helmholtz had believed that in the tone he had discovered 'the rigorously simple sonic sensation' out of which all sounds could be reconstructed by progressive combination. Mach's definition of the 'elements' is a philosophical extrapolation from these results: 'Physical nature is composed of the elements given by the senses. It is not things, objects, bodies, but rather colours, tones, pressures, spaces, times (what we usually call sensations) that are the true *elements* of the world,' from which he concluded: 'Everything mental is or will be divisible into elementary sensations. Now these elements of the inner world and those of the outer world *are the same.*'

One can see why Mach claimed, on this basis, to have resolved the question posed by the so-called 'disappearance of matter'. The question does not exist, he stated, since 'matter' has never in fact existed outside the brains of metaphysicians. . . .

[19] This philosophy is indeed both *empiricist* and *criticist*: empiricist insofar as Mach claims

Bogdanov took Mach at his word and stated: since this philosophy 'reconciles' materialism and idealism, by destroying the distinction between them, it is compatible with Marx's materialism. But the scientific conjuncture demands that Marxist philosophy be 'rejuvenated' if it is to be capable of explaining the latest results of the natural sciences. Hence one should have the courage to follow Engels's slogan that 'at each great scientific discovery materialism must change its form', and 'marry' it with empirio-criticism.

As is well known, this is the decisive point at which Lenin attacked in 1909: the division of philosophy between two tendencies is eternal, he recalled, also appealing to Engels, for, in the last analysis, it is based on the division of society into classes. Hence whatever he may say, Mach has in no way put an end to the conflict between materialism and idealism. Really, he is seeking to confuse the issue and conceal the fact that he is actually rallying to the idealist tendency in the history of philosophy, content to re-adopt its most worn-out themes beneath an apparently scientific modernist terminology. Moreover, his philosophy is by no means based on the results of the contemporary sciences, on the contrary, it is incompatible with the dominant tendency in them and should, along with its competitors among the other variants of idealist philosophy, be held responsible for the supposed 'state of crisis' of physics, which is no more than a philosophical crisis which has infected a few physicists at the moment when their science is undergoing a revolutionary change. And to complete his refutation, Lenin set out to prove that, inversely, the basic theses of dialectical materialism could help the physicists to formulate new concepts by enabling them to resist the encroachments of idealist philosophy onto their practice.

But there is one point in Bogdanov's system that Lenin is led to ignore by the logic of his argument,[20] a point which is of the greatest interest to us: that is the aspect in which this 'Russian

---

that all our knowledge, both of the external world and of ourselves, comes to us, via our sensations, from *experience*; criticist because, having posed this principle, he claims that our knowledge *is limited* to this content of our sensuous experience; it is therefore superfluous to imagine some cause for these sensations outside ourselves; the hypothesis is illegitimate, for under no circumstances could we know that cause save by our sensations; so it is to transgress our human condition in an illusory metaphysical movement to suppose that the external world is anything but an 'aspect' of our sensations.

[20] Lenin attacked in principle the notion of a possible 'adjustment' of Marxist philosophy to empirio-criticism; he therefore ignored the differences there are between Bogdanov and

disciple of Mach' states that he disagrees with his master. For if Bogdanov never failed to admit his debt to Mach, he never accepted the label 'Machist' for all that.

Now, Bogdanov saw the difference between his own system and that of Mach in what he called his 'monism'. In fact, throughout his work he constantly restated the ambition to 'complete' the 'monism' of which empirio-criticism was, for him, the most convincing although still inconsistent realization. It should be realized that this theme of 'monism' and the word for it go right back to his earliest philosophical options which he quite rightly linked to the 'materialism of the natural sciences' to which he had rallied initially and whose grip he was never fully to throw off.[21]

Monism was indeed the philosophical emblem and, it might be said, the 'slogan' of those whom Marx and Engels designated as 'vulgar materialists', most of them naturalists, adepts and popularisers of Darwinism, who had seen the theory of evolutionism as a source for anti-religious (even anti-clerical) and anti-metaphysical arguments.[22] These scientists and philosophers held in fact that everything in nature can be explained as a property of *matter*, without there being any need to resort to any transcendent element at all. Despite the fine differences between them, they had all made their own the famous maxim of the French doctor and ideologist Cabanis: 'The brain secretes thought as the liver secretes bile'.

From this 'monism', Bogdanov retained the project of presenting in his own philosophy (precisely empirio-*monism*) a 'general picture of the world' resting on a single principle of explanation based on a single origin for beings and things. It is by virtue of this

---

Mach, which are philosophically inessential anyway, to concentrate his analysis on Mach's philosophy and show why it is irreconcilable with Marxism because utterly idealist.

[21] In the preface to *Empirio-monism* Bodganov himself admits that it is a 'philosophy from which it is not easy to separate oneself'.

[22] The names of the main German 'vulgar materialists' are well known: Büchner, Vogt, Moleschott. 'Monism' was also proclaimed by Ernst Haeckel, the famous naturalist and Darwinist propagandist who exercised a profound influence on a whole generation. Because of its anti-religious aspect, 'monism' had been very popular in Russian populist milieux. As the reader will know, Plekhanov took up the terminology of monism to describe the Marxist conception of history. Stalin himself, in *Anarchism or Socialism*, presented Marxism as a monism. In the 1960's, Roger Garaudy, Gilbert Mury and Guy Besse believed that Marx's 'monism' could still be counterposed to Althusser's work, denounced as dualist. Really, as Dechezlepêtre has shown in an unpublished memoir, the mask of 'monism' has always concealed one of the constant attempts of the *'evolutionism'* which has been linked with it from the beginning to insinuate itself into Marxism.

presupposition that he undertook to criticize the empirio-criticist notion of experience, which he believed to be still afflicted with dualist contaminations.

Mach, he explained, was on the right lines when he emphasized in his notion of the 'element' the primary lack of differentiation between the 'physical' and the 'mental'. But he only went half-way and, a victim of his positivism, held to a narrowly descriptive point of view, observing the *fact* without seeking to explain the *why*, thus ultimately letting the principle of the *unity* of matter and mind escape him.

Bogdanov therefore attacked the question of the 'why' and altered the 'Machist' notion of experience accordingly, defining it as 'experience *of labour*'. This is the neuralgic point of Bogdanov's system, its secret spring, the key in the last analysis, although this is hardly yet foreseeable in *Empirio-monism*, to its subsequent political career. This 'correction' of Mach's thesis is indeed of some consequence, for it introduced into Bogdanov's system an element of internal imbalance which was to carry on developing its contradictory effects right up to *Tectology*.

In fact it is obvious, if one thinks about it, that the introduction of the notion of 'labour' as the Origin of experience is in brutal conflict with the very foundations of empirio-criticism, which was based on a sensualist conception of experience as a complex of *sensations* and which saw its philosophical triumph and its scientific guarantee in its successful disengagement of the notion of element from a pure analysis of simple sensations. To regard this 'analysis' as inadequate, as Bogdanov did, is thus to go against the very principle of empirio-criticism. So in a sense Bogdanov was not unjustified in his annoyance that his opponents simply assimilated his system to Mach's philosophy.

By my 'monism', by the construction of the unprecedented notion of 'experience of labour', I am, he claimed, in a position to base my doctrine on the 'social materialism' of Marx, which I regard as the scientific theory of the historical development of the forms of labour.

Here it is essential to pay close attention, for once again in a sense it can be said that Bogdanov was not unjustified: by introducing the notion of labour as basis for his conception of knowledge, he took a path that might have let him recognize, as a materialist, the primacy of practice over theory, and then forced him to abandon the empiricist category of experience which was his starting point and conceive knowledge as a *practice*; a theoretical practice in which, as Marxists do in fact maintain, primacy is accorded to practical (technical) knowledge over theoretical knowledge; a theoretical practice which itself, in its relative autonomy, is determined in the last instance by the practice of the production of material goods.

And in fact, Bogdanov, 'forgetting' his Machist philosophy – as Lenin remarked – quite often subsequently allowed himself to be won over by this tendency of his theoretical apparatus. To corroborate this, read the concrete analyses he made of the history of the sciences, particularly that of astronomy; or his remarkable critical analyses of the capitalist division of scientific labour and its effects: pages whose astonishing up-to-dateness has quite rightly been pointed out;[23] these pages in which the empiricism dwindles to the point of imperceptibility are in the last analysis an after-effect of the philosophical violence done to Mach's theses by the introduction of the notion of labour 'into' them.

But if on occasion he did in this way forget his basic philosophical reference point (Mach), Bogdanov never abandoned it. Which produced a really astounding result; it turns out in fact that this self-proclaimed Marxist theorist, who had written the preface to the first Russian edition of *Capital* (1909), was forced to turn his back on Marxism and think the notion of labour not in the Marxist terms of a *labour process* inserted into a production process which takes place in certain relations of production and is hence always marked by the class struggle, but in the Machist terms of *a biological process of the adaptation of the organism to its environment*.[24] So that in his works the main theoretical emphasis in the expression 'experience of labour' *is always ultimately on the term 'experience'*.

Hence the presence in Bogdanov's work, 'alongside' the concrete analyses I have just mentioned, but surmounting them theoretically and 'taking over' all their results in a resolutely idealist sense, of a genetic theory of scientific concepts and a continuist-evolutionist theory of the history of the sciences.

[23] As by Giulio Giorello in the preface he has written to the Italian translation of the pamphlet on *Science and the Working Class*, Bompiani, Milan 1974.

[24] Via the notion of *adaptation*, king-pin of the Machist theory of history, Bogdanov's 'monist' evolutionism can easily be brought into harmony with Mach's pragmatist 'evolutionism'.

The article called 'Methods of Labour and Methods of Knowledge' (1918) is probably the best illustration of this 'return' of
Machism in Bogdanov's work.

What, he asks, is the 'soul' of science? Answer: its methods: 'The
methods of science, i.e., the means thanks to which it works out
the truth, are the soul of science, the basis of its achievements.'[25]
Now, though apparently diverse, these methods can all be reduced
to *one* fundamental method: *induction*.[26] But what is the *origin* of
induction, asks Bogdanov? It is, he claims, the organism's adapta-
tional response to its environment, proceeding from a mere reflex
movement to what he calls a 'practical generalization'. This
generalization remains embryonic in the animal, but in man it
undergoes an extraordinary development, because man is a 'being
of labour' who has to organize means to an end. . . .

But clearly this explanation is not enough to explain how one
gets from practical generalization to *theoretical* generalization,
which is what induction really means. So we find Bogdanov
endeavouring to cobble together a theory of the common origin of
language and thought in the act of labour. Basing himself on the
works of the German monist philologist Noiré – the 'brilliant
Noiré', 'a Marxist in philology without knowing it'[27] – he defends
the notion that every *word* is always already from the beginning a
'word-concept' in the rudimentary form of a 'labour interjection'[28]
which constitutes 'the intelligible designation of the act of labour
to which it relates and which is natural to all the members of the
collectivity'. From which, finally, he can conclude that 'since the
original word signifies an action, a series of words already constituted a *technical rule*'. He has brought it off: all that now has to be
done is to describe the development of man's struggle against the

---

[25] As is well known, this positivist thesis of the *primacy of method* over concepts and
theories was to have an illustrious future in Marxist philosophy itself, where it is expressed
in the idealist thesis of the primacy of dialectics conceived as the Universal Method over
materialism.

[26] As we shall see, Bogdanov presents deduction as a derived form of induction.

[27] Thanks to the generosity, erudition and sagacity of Mlle. Y. Conry, I can identify
Ludwig Noiré (1829–89), who, as Bogdanov greatly regretted, has failed to leave an
imperishable name in the history of philology. A philosopher and philologist, he taught at
Mainz. He was the author of several works on the monist philosophy of language, of an
essay on Max Müller, from whom he took the term *interjection*, and of a historical introduction to an edition of the *Critique of Pure Reason* (1883).

[28] See the extraordinary passages of anthropology-fiction that Bogdanov devotes to this
question, such as *Methods of Labour and Methods of Knowledge* (1918).

environment to move from a lower stage of generalization to a higher stage, science thus appearing as the ultimate term in a continuous and progressive series.

Hence Bogdanov's doubly *anti-dialectical* thesis that 'ordinary thought' and 'scientific' thought are essentially the same, that there is no 'leap' between them and that 'scientific thought is only distinguished by its more organized aspect, i.e., by systematically rejecting everything which is contradictory'.

Logically one can but draw from this thesis *relativistic* epistemological conclusions as to the status of the truths produced by science. And this is what Bogdanov does, without hesitation; as the theoretician of the Universal System of all possible systems, he knows what consistency means. So he does not hesitate to write: the notion of 'objective truth' is a (metaphysical) 'fetish', for science has only ever produced 'epochal truths'. And when Plekhanov sharply reminded him that Engels had written exactly the opposite, maintaining that scientific truths are *objective* truths, he bridles, denounces bourgeois objectivism, maintains that his position is a Marxist one and attempts to prove that Engels could not have meant what he wrote! So true is it, for him, that the only Marxist definition of science is his one which 're-establishes the continuity of the bond between labour and science': 'science is the collective experience of organized labour'. Whence follows immediately a definition of truth as the *'organizing form of experience'*, obviously subject to the historical relativity of the 'data' of that 'experience'.

Sworn enemy of all contradiction, Bogdanov was never able to understand the Marxist position on this question. Despite Lenin's repeated explanations in *Materialism and Empirio-criticism*, he always refused to see the *dialectical* bond that unites, in what is in fact a *contradictory* unity, the relative and the absolute in dialectical-materialist theses; the theses that propose that the process of knowledge produces truths each of which, with respect to absolute truth, is historically only a relative truth, but is still absolutely a truth for all that.

We shall see how it was this anti-dialectical position that was to make Bogdanov the first to hold the theory of the 'two sciences' – bourgeois and proletarian – whose subsequent destiny is only too well known. . . .

But before turning to this burning issue, it is worth noting how Bogdanov's epistemological relativism is, as I have said, built onto a continuist and evolutionist theory of the history of the sciences.

If the soul of science is its methods; if these methods can all be reduced to their origin in methods of labour, the development of science must be related to that of the methods of labour. Once again ignoring the abstract character of the Marxist notion of the 'labour process', Bogdanov reduces the process of production to a progressively improving handling of the material elements of the productive forces alone; the level of improvement – 'organization' – of these elements expressing that of man's adaptation to his environment. The reference he makes on several occasions in this connection to Darwin should not conceal the fact that this is no more than a hybrid evolutionism, appealed to simply to justify Bogdanov's continuist and teleological thesis about the history of the sciences: that it is 'an uninterrupted chain of developments that runs from the elementary organizational procedures of labour to the summit of scientific methods'.

This thesis finds a place in what has to be called the idealist philosophy of history constructed by Bogdanov after *Empirio-monism*, which is itself an evolutionist philosophy of a quasi-Spencerian type, and which attempts to pass itself off as Marxist by making a mechanistic interpretation of the conceptions advanced by Marx of the productive forces, the relations of production and the relations between them. Indeed, it is very striking that in amputating the Marxist concept of 'productive forces' from its social-human element – labour power – and thus destroying the specific difference that separates this concept once and for all from any bourgeois technicist notion of technique, Bogdanov reduced the relations of production in their turn to *purely technical relations of organization of labour*. From then on, in his picture of the world, it is no longer, as it is with Marx, the class struggle which is the motor of all history, but rather the development of technique.[29] It has to be said that for Bogdanov, as later for Stalin, 'technique decides everything'. As a result, the division of society into classes seems only a transitory and inessential obstacle to the harmonious development of society in a temporally continuous and homo-geneous line, endowed with an inner purpose in the shadow cast by its Origin.

[29] Like Stalin later, and so many others since, Bogdanov bases himself on a mechanistic interpretation of the famous but theoretically ambiguous 1859 *Preface* to *A Contribution to the Critique of Political Economy*.

Thus the theoretical elements come together to form the grandiose system of *Tectology* that crowns this philosophy of history by describing the history of human societies as governed from the moment they emerged by a hitherto unnoticed principle of *organization*. Through the struggles and tragedies of real history,[30] Organization, an atemporal ordering principle, is what is seeking its realization. So that class societies – in particular, bourgeois society – are conceived as imperfect realizations or rough drafts of Organization; organizations whose principle – disorganization or 'anarchy' – betrays their own essence. By the same token they are revealed as fragile, unstable social formations, destined to disappear, because they were undermined from the very first by the silent contradiction which will carry them off.

Hence the Bogdanovist theory of proletarian revolution conceived not as a process of suppression of class struggle by class struggle, but as the advent of the originary essence of 'society as such', in the actual presence of a society of a new type, realizing in the end of all ends the Idea which had inhabited every previous society unbeknownst. As for the proletariat, far from being defined in this advent by the place that capitalist relations of production assign it in the class struggle, it is conceived as the bearer – I will go so far as to say the 'incarnation', for this is pure mysticism – of a project inscribed from the very beginning in the most embryonic forms of association between men. Its historical mission is to be, in Bogdanov's words, 'the class of organization'.

Hence finally an expressive conception of the social whole, whose essence – the technical forms of organization of labour – is equally manifested in each of its component parts. It is this expressive conception that governs the Bogdanovist theory of ideology; a theory Bogdanov always regarded as one of his essential contributions to the development of 'historical materialism'; a theory which did, indeed, in its way, seem to fill a gap in Marx's edifice.[31]

This theory is constructed around one central thesis, which the reader will already have guessed: ideology is the organization of

---

[30] Thus Bogdanov interprets 'hot-foot' the imperialist war of 1914 *and* the October Revolution in the same terms: as 'crises' of *disorganization* which should give rise to an organic period. We are very close to Saint-Simon and Auguste Comte, to utopian technocracy and bourgeois sociology.

[31] Many Marxists have been taken in by this theory, and not just minor ones, for Bukharin adopted it in his textbook *Historical Materialism*, citing Bogdanov on a number of occasions.

ideas that expresses at each moment of history the forms of organization of labour. It is understandable, given this basis, that Bogdanov should have proposed a *mechanistic* theory of ideological transformations which found a response in the idealist conception of ideology whose bearers had been the revolutionary intellectuals in Russia.[32]

3 The Bogdanovist Theory of the 'Two Sciences'

I leave it to the reader to discover and appreciate the tenacity and agility with which Bogdanov manages to assemble the disparate elements of his philosophical system into a theory which, as a good idealist, he makes applicable, willy-nilly, to everything either real or possible.

It is now time to examine one of his theses in a little more detail, an essential one, or at any rate the one which was destined to have the most resounding future: the thesis of the 'two sciences'. One cannot fail to note that the pages he devotes to it are profoundly marked by the contradiction which, as I have suggested, affects his basic philosophical armature. The introduction of the notion of labour into this armature as a foundation for the 'Machist' category of experience does allow him to break in one essential respect with the empiricist-positivist conception of science and produces in his theory the materialist effects which make his writings still absorbing today. But on the other hand, all his critical analyses of the bourgeois practice and conception of science are 'taken over' by his relativist conception of truth and his evolutionist conception of history, and it was precisely this takeover that gave rise to the construction of the notion of 'proletarian science'.

His criticism of 'bourgeois science' is developed on the basis of concrete examples in a pamphlet on *Science and the Working Class*.

As one might have expected, the criticism of contemporary

[32] If ideology is an expression of the forms of organization of labour, and if the workers of modern industry therefore express in their ideology the 'collectivist' essence of mechanized production, anticipations of the organization of the whole society and its ideology, then the ideology of the classes in alliance with them, notably the peasantry, which is profoundly individualistic, has to be destroyed. These theses simultaneously justify an economistic practice of ideological struggle which waits for the technical transformation of agricultural units to change peasant ideology (Bukharin's position, and, to a certain extent, Stalin's) and coercive methods against the peasants, especially in religious matters.

scientific practice is developed from the standpoint of its relation to labour. The bond originally, i.e., in his perspective *by nature*, linking science with labour has been broken in class societies, Bogdanov explains. Bourgeois science goes so far as to forget its origins completely, and all its faults and all its troubles should be imputed to this forgetfulness.

The first effect of this forgetfulness is that science has lost sight even of the idea of the unity of its methods and disintegrated into a disparate body of specialized disciplines each of which develops in ignorance of its neighbours, deprived of the concourse by which they could mutually reinforce one another. This *specialization*, which Bogdanov prosecutes at every opportunity, is denounced both as an effect and as an image within science of the *anarchy* reigning in capitalist production and little by little affecting the whole of bourgeois society. This specialization reinforces a tendency inherent in the status of science in all class societies which 'fetishizes' the results it obtains as so many 'sacred mysteries', stating them in an esoteric language inaccessible to the mass of the people. And these mysteries, adds Bogdanov, are all the more protected insofar as scientific methods, grudgingly revealed in a profoundly 'elitist' pedagogy, are jealously kept secret by those who know them. All this, he concludes, has helped to constitute a caste of 'mental aristocrats', academic grandees in the service of the holders of power.[33] Science has thus become an 'authoritarian' instrument of the rule of the exploiting classes.

So true is this that all those from among the oppressed who, by superhuman efforts, chance to get to share in these 'mysteries' are *ipso facto* distanced from their class brothers and often turned against them. 'Bourgeois science,' as Bogdanov constantly repeats, clearly obsessed by the question, 'is a science which makes bourgeois.'

The tasks of the proletariat where science is concerned are defined by these conditions. The slogan is, of course, first to re-establish the

[33] It is not surprising that this thesis received such a warm welcome from the revolutionary intelligentsia during the early years of the revolution, for most famous Russian scientists were hostile to the Soviet regime. This was the case in the natural sciences, for example, where, as A. Haudricourt recalled, a man such as Vavilov, who was devoted to the Soviet regime, was surrounded by specialists originating from the aristocracy who had nothing but hostility for the rabble. One of the reasons for Lysenko's rise was that he could play on the resultant mistrust of the academic authorities. He achieved this by placing himself under the banner of Ivan Michurin, whom he called the 'barefoot scientist'.

link between science and labour, which means in particular to rely on the collective basis of labour in mechanized production so as to fight the individualist ideology of the possessors of knowledge, to reform the language of science, simplifying and unifying it, so as to secure, not its vulgarization – for vulgarization always distorts its content as a function of the ideological aims of the ruling class – but its real *diffusion*; to recast pedagogy, lastly, simplifying it and bringing it into contact with practice. The result will be what Bogdanov calls a 'socialization' of scientific learning, promising an unprecedented future growth of knowledge.

These are fascinating pages, in which Bogdanov is not afraid to go into the technical – and notably pedagogic – details of the reforms he is putting forward, and in which we can still all find something useful to us today; they describe concretely what Marx abstractly designated in *Capital* as the 'enrolment of science in the service of capital'; they outline precisely the tasks of a possible 'proletarian organization of scientific research' as the effect on that research of a cultural revolution.

It must be admitted that the essence of the theses Bogdanov sustains on the effects of the capitalist division of scientific labour within that labour itself; on the conditions of its reproduction and the forms of its diffusion, and hence on its ideological function in the service of the dominant ideology, are perfectly compatible with the classical Marxist thesis of the objectivity of scientific knowledges. For this objectivity thesis must not be confused with the positivist thesis of the *neutrality* of science, as it is by some people, so eager to dispense with Marxism that they fail to understand its simplest philosophical statements. It should even be added that only the *thesis* of objectivity, insofar as it is a thesis that *poses* the objectivity of scientific truths *against* idealist bourgeois philosophies which make that objectivity subject to the legal question of its 'title' and its 'foundation', only this thesis enables one to formulate scientifically the problems of the history of scientific practice in its relations with other practices, and hence with the various forms of the class struggle.

The example of Bogdanov himself proves this *a contrario*: for hardly had he picked the fruits of the thesis of the primacy of practice over theory implied by his beginnings of a break with the 'Machist' category of 'experience'; hardly had he thus opened up to investigation the field of problems made thinkable by the thesis of objectivity, an objectivity that the first thesis contains as an obligatory consequence, than he was forced by his attachment to Mach's basic philosophical apparatus and the relativism linked to it into a contradiction with his own positions and the evasion of an 'ultra-left' idealist conception of 'proletarian science' as the only science in the full sense of the term.

In fact, it can be said that all the effects of Bogdanov's idealist positions converged to 'produce' this theory: if there are only 'epochal truths', all of the objectivity of which amounts to an expression of the level of development of the productive forces; if that level of development is always conveyed in the form of organization of the elements of the technique of labour; if those forms of organization are historically arranged according to a process of increasing rationalization and expansion in conformity with an evolution naturally based in 'biological' data; if, with 'mechanized production', the collectivism of those forms of organization seems to promise an extension of this finally universalized rationality to the whole of society; then it must be admitted that the working class is by itself, through its position in production and the vision allowed it of the whole of nature and society, the bearer of a new – 'universal' – 'point of view' which should enable it to recast completely the conceptual edifice of all the existing sciences.

Hence the famous lines from the pamphlet *Science and the Working Class*: 'To say that the class character of science resides in the *defence of the interests* of a given class is only a pamphleteer's argument or a falsification pure and simple. In reality, science may be bourgeois or proletarian in its very "nature", notably in *its origins, its conceptions, its methods of study and exposition*. In this fundamental sense, all the sciences, social or otherwise, including mathematics and logic, can have and really do have a class character.'

Hence, finally, the plan for a Proletarian University, and the attempts to realize it in the Socialist Academy, and then the projected edition of a *Workers' Encyclopedia*. A plan, attempts and a project that depend on the notion that the working class, the only class capable of theorizing on the basis of its practice the new collective-rational *methods* of mechanized production, is the bearer of a 'new logic', and hence promises a new science.[34]

---

[34] This Bogdanovist theme of a 'proletarian logic' is a stubborn growth: it has sprung up again recently and simultaneously in the works of Jacques Rancière, Jean-Marc Lévy-Leblond and Alain Badiou.

4   Bogdanovism in Stalinist Ideology

The history, most of it subterranean, of Bogdanovist themes is, I believe, indispensable to anyone who wishes to understand the constitution of the Soviet ideological system and the springs of the Stalinist practice of ideological struggle.

This history coincides at first with the 'public' history of the Proletkult. Now, as I have already said, it was because it successfully systematized the 'spontaneous' ideology of the Russian revolutionary intelligentsia, because it bound together, in a theory which claimed to range itself in the camp of Marxism, the sectarian, anti-peasant tendencies and the economistic-technocratic tendencies of this intelligentsia, that it made an immense and durable impression, Lenin notwithstanding. It adequately expressed the specific form of the petty-bourgeois ideology that Russian intellectuals received from their history.

But that is not all, for we have to add a supplementary reason helping to strengthen its audience and to extend the range of its appeal beyond the social stratum of the intellectuals into the masses themselves; a reason which also in a sense helped to assure the survival of its essential themes. This reason is a simple, but strong one: it is that many of the questions that Bogdanov posed in a mystified and contradictory way in his 'tectological' system reflected in their own way questions which the revolutionary process objectively *put on the agenda* at the same moment: the questions posed by the necessity for a 'cultural revolution', as Lenin called it, in order to pursue the socialist transition towards communism after the seizure of state power by the proletariat.

Listen for a moment to the Proletkult militants. How, they ask, are we to construct a new culture which 'corresponds' to the new relations of production? Should we or should we not make a 'tabula rasa' of the works of the past, or would it be better, as Marx suggested enigmatically, to appropriate its 'heritage' in a critical way? And a question which dominated the rest and was at stake in struggles of unprecedented bitterness in these days when all seemed possible: what new forms should be invented for education and pedagogy? Was it enough to send the children of workers to the schools instituted in the Tsarist regime? Should not educational institutions be modified and pedagogic methods be recast in the perspective of an end to the division between manual and mental labour, the perspective of communism? More generally, how should the effects of the revolution be brought to bear on the every-day life of the masses, how should one practically challenge what in Russia is called '*byt*', i.e., in Marxist terms, the set of concrete ideological relations?

Now, in all these burning issues, Marxist theory fell dramatically short, deprived as it still was of a sufficiently developed notion of ideological transformations. Bogdanov thus filled a gap with his doctrine; in these questions left unanswered by Marxism he found the necessary theoretical basis for his success.

Lenin was perfectly well aware of this situation, and if, as we have seen, he was not sparing in his criticisms of the Boganovist notion of 'proletarian culture'; if, for the reasons and in the forms I have described, he took measures to bring the Proletkult's expansion to a stop, he never failed to stress that the questions of 'cultural revolution' and in particular of the reorganization of the educational apparatus were open questions vitally interesting and urgent for the revolution.

Stalin's procedure, on the other hand, was quite different: he simply buried these questions, before officially burying the Proletkult itself. But at the same time he managed to take advantage of the ambiguities implicit in their formulation and hence in the Bogdanovist perspective. He thus enclosed all ideological and cultural questions in the theoretical *limits* which had restricted the Proletkult itself. And as these theoretical limits were ultimately an expression of the petty-bourgeois ideology of the theoreticians of that movement, he was able to use the answers as a means to unify the stratum of intellectuals, production specialists and cadres in the state apparatus which was constantly reinforced by his economistic-technicist policy and required by his practices of repression. The Proletkult's themes were thus confiscated to serve an 'official' propaganda whose pragmatic aims were remote from the dreams of those well-meaning militants. This was already illustrated in 1928 at the time of the trial at Shakty in the Donbass of some engineers, bourgeois specialists accused of sabotage. The government decided, in its own words, to 'loosen the reins' on the cultural front – i.e., after years of silence imposed in the interests of the NEP, to allow former 'Proletkultists' to speak out. The movement this gave rise to was largely a spontaneous one, but the government was quickly able to take it over as a means of mobilizing the masses ideologically around its policy of collectivization. The fact is that for three years the Bogdanovist themes of voluntarist humanism re-emerged; but this time as elements of the official ideological discourse. The questions which had fuelled the movement of 1918 re-emerged at the same time, among them, naturally enough, that of the constitution of a 'proletarian science'. Thus, in the magazine *Pod Znamenem Marksizma*, for example, there is an article by V. P. Egorshin containing the following passage: 'The modern science of nature is also a class phenomenon, just as much as philosophy and art. . . . It is bourgeois in its theoretical foundations.' There then follows, word for word, the Bogdanovist project of a doctrinal and institutional 'recasting' of the sciences of nature subsequent to their critical re-examination; it constitutes the object of the specially created *Institute of Red Professors.*[35]

The outcome of this movement is revealing. It was a ban and a trick: in 1932, hardly had they redeployed on the 'front' of the ideological battle, the combatants were called on to withdraw in good order. The projects for a 'proletarianization' of the educational apparatus, which meant to the Komsomols and Pioneers who had adopted them the destruction of the old system and its replacement by a new type of institution which would have begun to reunite manual labour and intellectual labour, in fact resulted in decrees which subjected the existing educational system (with a few minor reforms) more closely to the authority of the Party. All that was alive in the attempts and organizations of the 'proletarian' writers was destroyed: there then began the period of the conformism and sectarianism of the Union of Writers. As for the natural sciences, the only original institution, officially set up in 1918 as the Socialist Academy and becoming the Communist Academy in 1923, was integrated into the Academy of Sciences as one of its specialized sections in 1936.

But the interesting thing about this is that hardly had Stalin proceeded to this bringing to heel than he accorded the ideological themes around which the movement had regrouped itself a kind of verbal resurrection. In 1935, he set the tone for the celebration of 'Socialist Man', 'a new man of a hitherto unknown species'; and from 1936 these themes were to become an integral and essential

---

[35] On all these points one can refer to the works of the American historian Sheila Fitzpatrick on the 'Soviet cultural revolution'.

part of the official ideology of the Soviet state. Until the War the real or imaginary exploits of the Stakhanovites provided ever new occasions for their reactivation and amplification. I have suggested elsewhere[36] how these themes were then made the 'foundation' for the veritable flight forward that Stalinist policy performed when confronted with the unprecedented problems posed by the forms of the class struggle in a transition period, and a mask, by denying the very existence of that struggle, for the coercive answers they were given.

The final official adoption, in 1948, of the theory of the 'two sciences' as a theme in the campaign which endorsed Lysenko's scientific frauds as state doctrine and in a few months spread to all cultural spheres, is surprising at first glance when one realizes that the Zhdanovists unleashed what they themselves called a 'Machist hunt', while taking their slogan ('bourgeois science *or* proletarian science'), without saying so, obviously, and probably without knowing it, from the theory of the man whom Lenin had denounced as 'Mach's Russian disciple'! But we can now understand what lay behind this apparent irony of history. The same ideological mechanism is at work in it. In a moment of crisis[37] when the Soviet Party and state needed to tighten the ranks of intellectuals around them in order that they fulfill their 'organic' function, and the ranks of the Communist Parties of the whole world around the Soviet Union in order to counter the plans of American imperialism, they revived the 'ultra-left' variant of the intellectuals' 'spontaneous' Bogdanovist ideology, now stowing it in the official version of Marxist philosophy.[38] With the notorious effects of intimidation, threat and repression within the Soviet Union and in the various Communist Parties of the 'imperialist camp' (even if in the latter the tragic consequences for individuals could not be so fateful as they were in the former).

[36] See pp. 75–77 above.

[37] An internal crisis affecting the Party's relationship with the masses once the patriotic fervour of the war years had died down and resort had once again been made to repressive practices; an external crisis overdetermining the internal one and corresponding to the 'turn' in Stalin's policy vis-à-vis his wartime 'allies'. A turn initiated by Zhdanov's report on the international situation of February 1947 which was to install the Soviet Union in the 'Cold War'.

[38] In my remarks on Lysenko above, I have briefly demonstrated how this 'ontological' version of dialectical materialism was in principle perfectly compatible with the 'Bogdanovist' theme of the two sciences, although the latter need not necessarily be deduced from it.

★ ★ ★

Can it be said that in this sort of petrified cultural revolution we have the last avatar of Bogdanovism in Soviet ideology, and that it then disappeared for ever along with the great Zhdanovist masquerade? Maybe. Yet is it really certain that the theme of '*the* scientific and technical revolution' which is one of the main themes of official Soviet ideology today and which, as an essential component of the so-called theory of 'state monopoly capitalism', wreaks its political and theoretical havoc in the Western Communist Parties, is alien to the presuppositions of this system? A system still the victim of à 'forgetfulness' whose tenacity, it must be admitted, is still decidedly symptomatic.

Index